# *RENEW YOUR MIND*

## *VOLUME TWO*

*Vivian Daniels*

# Contents

What is the definition of a mind? Actually, a mind can be defined as a person's set of intellectual or mental faculties. The 'human mind' refers to the group of cognitive psychiatric processes that includes functions like perception, memory and reasoning. Moreover, a mind is the element of a person that enables them to be aware of their world and their experiences, to think thoughts that run through the mind.

Another definition of mind: mind may refer to the aspects of intellect and consciousness manifested as combinations of thought, perception, memory, emotion, will and imagination, including all of the brain's conscious and unconscious cognitive processes of reason.

However, what exactly is the mind? Obviously, mind is about mental processes, thought and consciousness. Many theories have been put forward to explain the relationship between what you call your mind, defined as the conscious thinking which experiences your thought, and brain parts of your body. A common theory posits that the human brain is a complex adaptive system, composed of relatively specialised and domain generated adaptive responses to the environment. Literally our mind is a battlefield. Most likely of, which passeth all understanding, shall keep your hearts and minds through Christ Jesus. Obviously, our mind is powerful, it creates our reality. The devil is after our mind because our mind speaks who we are. The Bible said, if you renew your mind often, it enables you, to think as the Bible said, Finally, brethren peace of God, whatsoever things are true, whatsoever things are honest, wheresoever things are pure, whatsoever things are lovely, whatsoever are of a good report; if there be any virtue, and if there be any praise, think on these things. When you renew your mind. *Renew your mind* can be identified as:

to see a thing the way God sees it and not the way you see it in your own mind because our minds are always full with junk.

If you renew your mind, obviously it will enable you to change the way you think and it will help you to meditate on the word of God.

> JOSHUA 1 VS 8 This book of the law shall not depart out of thy mouth; but thou shalt meditate therein day and night that thou mayest observe to do according to all that is written therein; for then thou shalt make thy way prosperous, and then thou shalt have good success.

Actually, look at what God promises Joshua if he meditates on the word of God, you know God cannot lie, He said have not I commanded thee? Be strong and of a good courage; be not afraid neither be thou dismayed for the Lord thy God is with thee whithersoever thou goest.

> PROVERB 4 VS 23 Keep thy heart with all diligence; for out of it are the issues of life.

> ISAIAH 26 VS 3 Thou wilt keep him in perfect peace, whose mind is stayed in thee; because he trusteth in thee.

Very important. As a matter of fact, your mind can make you or destroy you. Whatever you feed your mind is equally very important. Moreover, when you have the right mind, it will enable you to influence your character and it will help you to handle situation right. Obviously, our mind is like a garden and your thought is the seed; it depends what you choose to plant there, good or bad. Actually, when you renew your mind, it will enable you to discover what God promises you. However, your battles are won or lost in your mind before you started thinking of it. As a matter of fact, if you are defeated in your mind, it is difficult for you to win in the physical arena. Basically, see what happened when your mind is not renewed.

> NUMBERS 13 VS 31 to 33 But the men that went up with him said, we be not able to go up against the people; for they are stronger than we. Your only limit is you. And they brought up an evil report of the land which they had searched it, is a land that eateth up the inhabitants thereof; and all the people that we saw in it are men of a great stature. And there we saw the giants' sons of Anak, which come of the giants; and we were in our own sight as grasshoppers, and so we were in their sight. Obviously when your mind is renewed you see things differently.

> NUMBERS 13 VS 30 And Caleb stilled the people before Moses and said, Let us go up at once, and possess it; for we are well able to overcome it. Glory be to God. Actually, your mind can open a door for you or close a door for your future.

> ISAIAH 41 VS 9 to 12 Thou whom I have taken from the ends of the earth, and called thee from the chief men thereof, and said unto thee, thou art my servant; I have chosen thee, and not cast thee away. Fear thou not; for I am thy God; not dismayed; for I am thy God; I will strengthen thee; yea, I will uphold thee with the right hand of my righteousness. Behold, all they that were incensed against thee shall be ashamed and confounded; they shall be as nothing; and they

that strive with thee shall perish. Thou shalt seek them, and shalt not find them, even them that contented with thee; they that war against thee shall be as nothing, and as a thing of nought. Hallelujah.

ACTS 20 VS 32 And now, brethren commend you to God, and to the word of his grace, which is able to build you up and give you an inheritance among all them which are sanctified. Hallelujah.

However, there is another thing in life about your mind, you can decide to plant seeds of Abundance, Positivity, and Love or you can plant seeds of Regret, Negativity, Lack. That is why you have to renew your mind continually. Your mind is very important, that is why the devil attacks your mind. Moreover, we picture things with our mind before we start our planning and whatever we see and accept shapes our life. Wherefore, gird up the loins of your mind, be sober, and hope to the end for the grace that is to be brought unto you at the revelation of Jesus Christ. Obviously, that is why I emphasize for you to renew your mind continually. Our mind is a very important tool that so busy at all times. Basically, see what Apostle Paul said, now then it is no more I that do it, but sin that dwelleth in me. For I know that in me that is, in my flesh, dwelleth no good thing; for to will is present with me; but how to perform that which is good I find not. For the good that I would I do not; but the evil which I would not, that I do. Now if I do that I would not, it is no more I that do it, but sin that dwelleth in me. For I know that in me – that is, in my flesh – dwelleth no good thing; for to will is present with me; but how to perform that which is good I find not. For the good that would I do not; that I do. Now if

I do that I would not, it is no more I did it, but sin that dwelleth in me. **[ROMANS 7 VS 17 TO 20]**

Actually, be careful what you feed your mind because your mind shapes your life.

> ROMANS 12 VS 1 AND 2 I beseech you therefore, brethren, by the mercies of God, that ye present your bodies a living sacrifice holy acceptable unto God, which is your reasonable service. And be not conformed to this world; but be ye transformed by the renewing of your mind, that ye may prove what is that good and acceptable and perfect will of God.

Obviously, everything starts with your mind; feed your mind with ability so that any problem you face you can handle it. So, anything you can conceive, you can achieve it, because every production is a version of your mind. Actually, we are the seed of Abram, the world belongs to us, it doesn't matter which country we are in, with a right mind we can achieve our goals. Moreover, your mind plays an important role in achieving every kind of success and goal. Eventually, it is your mind that creates your world. Certainly, it is not your world that determines your world, it is your mind that determines your world. As a matter of fact, no matter how good your external environment, a bad mindset will destroy it. Actually, the mind governed by flesh is death, but mind governed by the spirit of God is life and peace. The word Holy Spirit is the non-anxious presence of God working in your life, that is why you have to renew your mind every day. Let this mind be in you, which was also in Christ Jesus. And be renewed in the spirit of your mind and that ye put on the new man, which after God is created in righteousness and true holiness. Literally when your mind is renewed it enables you to see things differently and you will develop a positive character and not be negative. Definitely, when your thought is right, fear will vanish away because your mind is renewed. When your mind is renewed it will enable you to set your mind on things above not on earthly things. Moreover, when your mind is renewed, it will enable you to ask God: create in me a clean heart O, God and renew a steadfast spirit within me. Victory is defeated in the picture of your mind; our mind is an important tool God has given to us. Moreover, your mind helps you to channel all your focus. Obviously, so many don't know the use of their mind. If your mind is disciplined, it will help you to stay focussed. Actually, you have to develop Kingdom mindset. Basically, the quality of your thinking determines the quality of your life. Remember, you are your thought, you are the way you think. As a matter of fact, the problem we have in this world is because we have people without transforming minds. Transform your mind, change your brain by the way you think.

> COLOSSIANS 3 VS 2 to 4 Set your affection on things above, not on things on the earth. For you are dead, and your life is hiding with Christ in God. When Christ; who is our life, shall appear; then shall ye also appear with him in glory.

> PSALM 51 VS 10 Create in me a clean heart O God; and renew a right spirit within me.

> ROMANS 8 VS 6 For to be carnally minded is death; but to be spiritually minded is life and peace.

> ISAIAH 43 VS 18 To 19 Remember ye not the former things, neither consider the things of old.

Behold will do a new thing; now it shall spring forth; shall ye not know it will even make a way in the wilderness; and rivers in the desert.

Obviously, the word of God said, be not conformed to this world, but be ye transformed by the renewing of your mind. Be careful for nothing; but in everything by prayer and supplication with thanksgiving let your requests be made known unto God. And the peace of God, which passeth understanding, shall keep your hearts and minds though Christ Jesus.

Actually, a man's life is what his thoughts make of it. However, when you want to change the outside, you first of all change your inside because we start to create things inside our minds. As a matter of fact, our thoughts create our reality; most likely, the way we behave and act defines who we are and what we experience in life. For instance the way you behave and act is simply a construction of how you think and feel; and emotions are reactions of the thoughts you give attention to. Obviously, you must be careful the attention you give to thoughts because what you think directly influences how you feel and how you feel directly influences how your body reacts. Almighty God said: Forget the former things; do not dwell on the past. See, I am doing a new thing. As a matter of fact, if you renew you mind, and ask God for a vision, or to enlarge the one He's already given you, you need to make room mentally.

2 CORINTHIANS 4 VS 16 For which cause we faint not; but though our outward man perish, yet the inward man is renewed day by day.

Paul said his inward man was renewed day by day. Very important because our mind is in a battlefield not a fun fair. Basically, you have to renew your mind always because your mind moves fast; that is why you have learned how to control your mind. As a matter of fact, man's failure started with his mind, which is why the Bible said: as you thinketh in his heart so he is. Victory is defeated in the picture you see in your mind. When your mind is sharp, it makes you not to cry for anybody because you mind is in the right place. When it is renewed.

*Renew your mind* is crucial and part of living a successful life. However, there are few principles that will help you better understand the concept of *renew your mind*; First, understand that God is not willing that any should perish. Not only is it His will for you to be saved but it is also His will for you to be free so you can know what is good and acceptable and the perfect will of God for your life. Obviously, you need to know that God reveals his will for mankind through his word. Moreover, as you study and put God's word into practice you will come to understand God's will for your life. Although when your mind is renewed, there is no obstacle too hard for you, and when you stay focussed, you will achieve your goal. Moreover, *renew your mind* will enable you to see any challenges as opportunities. Most likely you will achieve the greatness that is in you, Glory be to God.

> *"There are no great men, only challenges those ordinary men are forced to meet"*
>
> **William E Halsey**

ISAIAH 55 VS 8 That is why God said: my thoughts are not your thoughts, neither are your ways my ways, saith the Lord. For as the heavens are higher than your ways, and my thoughts than your thoughts.

Enlarge the place of your tent, stretch your tent curtains, strengthen your stakes. For you will spread out to the right and to the left.

ROMANS 12 VS 2 And be not conformed to this world; but be ye transformed by the renewing of your mind, that ye may prove what is that good and acceptable, and perfect will of God,

PHILIPPIANS 4 VS 6 Be careful for nothing; but in everything by prayer and supplication with thanksgiving let your requests be made unto God.

Literally, if you can change your thought, you will change your feeling as well and you will also eliminate the triggers that set off those feelings. As a matter of fact, you are the control of your thought, it will either bring you up or bring you down However, if you can control your thought, you will become a master of your mind because your mind is the engine room of your body. Your mind is the powerful tool you have for the creation of good in your life. However, if not used correctly, it can also be the destructive force in your life. Obviously, for you to control your thought means to influence the way you live your life. Most likely you only conquer and achieve by your thought. By good and bad thought you will repeat your harvest. As a matter of fact, the way you care for yourself determines how far you will create your future because if you cannot see far, you cannot go far. However, what controls your mind, controls your life.

> JOB 22 VS 18 to 23 Yet he filled their house with things; but the counsel of the wicked is far from me. The righteous see it, and are glad and the innocent laugh them to scorn. Whereas our substance is not cut down, but the remnant of them the fire consumeth. Acquaint now thy thyself with him and be at peace; thereby good shall come unto thee. Receive I pray thee, the law from his mouth, and lay up his words in thine heart. If thou return to the Almighty, thou shalt be built up, thou shalt put away iniquity far from thy tabernacles. Then shalt thou lay-up gold as dust and the gold of Ophir as the stones of the brooks. Yet, the Almighty shalt be thy defence, and thou shalt have plenty of silver.

Consider this! You are today what you believed about yourself yesterday, and you will be tomorrow what you believe about yourself right now. Joel Osteen

Obviously *renew your mind* is the key.

## LET US PRAY

Our father and our God, unto thee, O Lord do we lift up our soul. God, we trust in you. Don't let us be ashamed, and let not our enemies' triumph over us, as we wait on thee. Shew us thy ways O Lord and teach us thy paths. Almighty God lead us to thy truth, and teach us, for thou art the God of our salvation; on thee do we wait all the day. Almighty God remember thy tender mercy and thy loving kindnesses; for they have been of ever of old. My God and my Lord remember not the sins of our youth, nor my transgressions; according to thy mercy, remember thou us for thy goodness's sake O Lord. Our eyes are ever toward the Lord. Lord, pluck our feet out of their net. Turn to us and have mercy upon us; for we are desolate and affected. The troubles of our hearts are enlarged; My God and my Lord bring us out of distresses in Jesus Christ we pray. Amen.

Our man of God said: the words 'mind' and 'heart' are used interchangeably in the Bible, particularly in the Old Testament. However, the mind is the centre of human activity. Again, we must reiterate that the human mind is the most amazing phenomenon in the life of a man. It is that which gives us ability to think, reason, to achieve great inventions, to conceive great ideas. The power of the human mind is underestimated. It is argued that even the best of men only use ten percent of their minds. What the human mind conceives can be achieved. That is why our conception must be centred on the Word of God. He said your thoughts create your realities. As a matter of fact, your encounters in life are a product of your own mindset.

> 1 CORINTHIANS 3 VS 16 For who hath known the mind of the Lord, that he may instruct him. But we have the mind of Christ.

Basically, you need to take control of your mind by not using negative words. Moreover, your mind is more than mere imaginations; your mind is a mental picture with constructions or destructive capabilities. As a matter fact with your mind you can create a lot of things if you use it right. Actually, do you know that the mental construction of your mind is based on your imagination, it has the power to keep your bondage or to liberate you, to be a better person. That is why you have to protect your mind by renew it day by day according to Apostle Paul's advice.

Literally, as you are renewing your mind, don't allow any negative people to steal your Joy. However, when you lose your joy, you lose your strength because they will not understand you again – you are now at another level – and they don't see what you see. Look at what Jesus said to his disciples: And he turned him unto his disciples, and said privately, blessed are the eyes which see the things that ye see. As a matter fact, when your mind is renewed, it will enable you to stay positive and confident and you will achieve your goal. Moreover, develop your mind, think in a right perspective and continually update your mind. Study and meditate on God's word for yourself.

> LUKE 10 VS 21 to 23 In that hour Jesus rejoiced in spirit and said, thank thee, O Father Lord of heaven and earth that thou hast hid these things from the wise and prudent, and hast revealed them unto babes. Even so, Father, for so it seemed good in thy sight. All things are delivered to me of my Father; and no man knoweth who the Son is, but the Father; and who the Father is, but the Son, and he to whom the Son will reveal him. And he turned him unto his disciples, and said privately; Blessed are the eyes which see the things that ye see, Hallelujah.

> 2 TIMOTHY 2 VS 15 Study to shew thyself approved unto God, a workman that needeth not to be ashamed, rightly dividing the word in truth.

## LET US PRAY

Our Lord and our God, you are our light and our salvation, whom shall we fear? Our Lord you are our strength of our life. My Lord of whom shall we be afraid? Our trust is in you Lord, when the wicked even our enemies and our foes, came upon us to eat up our flesh, they stumbled and fell. My Father and our Lord, even though the host should encamp against us, our heart shall not fear; Even though the war shall rise up against us, in you Lord we have our confidence because if you be for us, who can be against us? My Lord, one thing we desired of thee, to seek after you and we will dwell in the house of the Lord all the days of our life. My Lord, and our God, deliver us not into the will of our enemies because false witnesses have risen against us. My Lord in the time of trouble, you shall hide us in his pavilion in the secret of his tabernacle shall you hide us, in Jesus' name we pray. Our Lord we are forgotten as a dead people out of mind; We are like a broken vessel. Moreover, we have heard the slander of many and fear was on every side; while they took counsel together against us., they devised to take away our life. However, Lord our life is trusted in thee. O Lord, we said, thou are our God. Our times are in thy hand, deliver us from the hands of our enemies and from them that persecute us. O Lord and our God make thy face to shine upon thy children, save us for thy mercy's sake. Amen.

Actually, if you build your mind, you will build everything. As a matter fact, if you build your mind, it will enable a change in your story because your mind is developed and you are seeing a new you. Moreover, when you renew your mind and build it up you will succeed but a mind that is not built and renewed will not succeed. However, if you don't have mental toughness, you cannot achieve anything in life. Obviously, if you don't renew your mind, you will remain a victim of stumbling blocks. When our mind wanders about most of the time, that is why it leans toward negative thoughts. Moreover, without interceding it can lead you to negativity. Literally, one motivational speaker by name Zig Ziglar said: what you picture in your mind, your mind will go to work to accomplish it. Indeed, when you change your pictures, you automatically change your performance. Hallelujah. Actually, you have to realise that each person is the principal factor that determines success in their life, that is why you have to think right, and stop thinking problems and stop thinking impossibilities. Most likely you must watch what goes into your mind, just be aware of what you think because you are what you think. However, you know God cannot do anything without your mind, your mind is as important as your spirit.

> PHILEMON 1 VS 14 But without thy mind would I do nothing; that thy benefit should not be as it were of necessity, but willingly.

> ISAIAH 65 VS 16 TO 24 That he who blesseth himself in the earth shall bless himself in the God of truth; and he that sweareth in the earth shall swear by the God of truth; because the former troubles are forgotten, and because they are hid from mine eyes. For, behold, I create new heavens and a new earth: and the former shall not be remembered, nor come into mind. But be ye glad and rejoice for ever in that which I create: for, behold, I create Jerusalem a rejoicing, and her people a joy. And I will rejoice in Jerusalem, and joy in my people: and the voice of weeping shall be no more heard in her, nor the voice of crying. There shall be no more thence an infant

of days, nor an old man that hath not filled his days: for the child shall die an hundred years old; but the sinner being an hundred years old shall be accursed. And they shall build houses, and inhabit them; and they shall plant vineyards, and eat the fruit of them. They shall not build, and another inhabit; they shall not plant, and another eat: for as the days of a tree are the days of my people, and mine elect shall long enjoy the work of their hands. Amen.

However, Satan always attacks our mind, even our Lord Jesus, Satan attacked him by telling him: if thou be the son of God, command these stones to be bread. Devil took Him up into the holy city and setteth on a pinnacle of temple and saith unto him; if thou be the son if God, cast thy self down. But Jesus answered and said unto him: it is written, thou shall not tempt the Lord thy God because his mind is renewed. He knew who Satan was, a deceiver and a liar, seeking whom he will destroy and kill. Actually, nothing becomes a reality in the life of any man until his mind is able to accommodate it.

MATTHEW 2 VS 3 to 6 And when the tempters came to Him, and said if thou be the son of God command that these stones be made bread, but He answered and said it is written, man shall not live by bread alone, but by every word that proceeded out of the month of God. Then the devil taketh Him up into the holy city and setteth him on a pinnacle of the temple. And saith unto Him, if thou be the son of God, cast thy self down, for it is written, He shall give his angels charge concerning thee, and in their hands, they shall bear thee up, lest at any time thou dash thy foot against a stone. Jesus said unto him it is written again, thou shall not tempt the Lord thy God.

Obviously, that is why as Christians we have to renew our minds every day, by speaking the word of God in our spirits, knowing that our weapons of our warfare are not carnal but pulling down the strongholds, why will you do that? By renewing your mind because Satan is after your destiny. Actually, that is why he is attracting your mind. Moreover, if you fall by his lies, you will start seeing defeat, fear and failure. As a matter of fact, at that stage you start imaging what is going to happen to you. The devil is a liar. Moreover, that is why God said cast down and bring it into captivity into God's obedience. We are at war in this world. Literally, that is why God said that our weapons of our warfare are not carnal but mighty through God for the pulling down of strongholds. However, you have to realise that God makes everything out according to his plan. For instance, does it mean that Apostle Paul understood every detail of God's plan? O no, however, when he didn't understand the plan, he trusted the planner! Moreover, that's where Paul's peace, joy and contentment came from. Basically, the same is applicable to you. The almighty God withholds no good thing from those who do what is perfect in his sight. Hallelujah.

> 2 CORINTHIANS 10 VS 3 TO 5 For though we walk in the flesh, we do not war after the flesh. For the weapons of our warfare are not carnal, but mighty through God to the pulling down of strong holds; Casting down imaginations and every high that exalted itself against the knowledge of God, and bring into captivity every thought to the obedience of Christ.

1 TIMOTHY 6 VS 6 to 7 But godliness with Contentment is great gain. For we brought nothing into this world, and it is certain we can carry nothing out.

# CONFESSION

My Lord, we thank you for letting us know how to protect our mind, by not speaking any negative words by control of our mind and renewing it day by day. Moreover, if we renew our mind, it will transform us from glory to glory. Glory be to God almighty. Amen.

GOD BLESSING IF YOU BELIEVE AND IT WILL BE ONTO YOU IN JESUS NAME. AMEN.

LEVITICUS 26 VS 2 to 13 Ye shall keep my sabbaths, and reverence my sanctuary; I am the Lord. If ye walk in my statutes, and keep my commandment, and do them; Then I will give you rain in due season, and the land shall yield her increase, and the trees of the field shall yield their fruit. And your threshing shall reach unto the vintage, and the vintage shall reach unto the sowing time; and ye shall eat your bread to the full and dwell in your land safely. And I will give peace in the land and ye shall lie down, and none shall make you afraid; and I will rid evil beasts out of the land, neither shall the sword go through your land. And ye shall chase your enemies and they shall fall before you by the sword. And five of you shall chase an hundred and an hundred of you shall put ten thousand to flight; and your enemies shall fall before you by the sword. For I will have respect unto you, and make you fruitful, and multiply you, and establish my covenant with you. And ye shall eat old store, and bring forth the old because of the new. And I will set my tabernacle among you; and my soul shall not abhor you. And I will walk among you, and will be your God, and ye shall be my people. Am the Lord your God, which brought you forth out of the land of Egypt, that ye should not be their bondmen, and I have broken the bands of your yoke, and made you go upright, In Jesus name. God cannot lie. He is a covenant keeping God.

NUMBERS 23 VS 19 to 20 God is not a man, that he should lie; neither the son of man, that he should be repentant; he said, and shall he not do it? Or hath he spoken, and shall he not make it good? Be hold have received commandment to bless; and he hath blessed; and I cannot reverse it.

Praise God, God is not man, when he blesses, no man can take it from you. And He cannot lie. Hallelujah. However, look at what our almighty father said, He said if I bless, no man can take it from you and he cannot reverse it back. Hallelujah, just trust God and his word because he is not a man.

Actually, when your mind is renewed, there is no obstacle too hard for you; moreover, when you stay focused and not distracted about things of the world, as a matter fact you will achieve your goal. Moreover, if your mind is renewed you will see any challenges as opportunities, and you will achieve the greatness that is in you. Obviously, there is power in a quiet mind, because our creative mind is activated during times of mental quietness. John Maxwell gave his final thoughts by saying: "If you are not doing something with your life, it doesn't matter how long it is, If you are doing something with your life, it doesn't matter how long it is. Life does not come of years lived."

"There are no great men, only great challenges that ordinary men forced to meet." By William F. Halsey.

> PHILIPPIANS 4 VS 7 And the peace of God, which passeth all understanding, shall keep your hearts and minds through Christ Jesus.

> PSALM 50 VS 15 and 16 And call upon me in the day of trouble; I will deliver thee, and thou shalt glorify me. But unto the wicked God saith, What hast thou to do to declare my statutes, or that thou shouldest take my covenant in thy mouth?

## LET US PRAY FOR PEACE

Lord. Your word says: "Thou will keep him in perfect peace whose mind is stayed on thee, because he trusteth in thee." Your word says: "The Lord gives strength to his people; the Lord blesses his people with peace." Your word says: "Peace I leave with you; my peace I gives you. Do not let your heart be troubled and do not be afraid "Your word says, the peace of God, which transcends all understanding will guard your hearts and your mind in Christ Jesus name." Amen.

My Lord, we need this peace which transcends understanding to settle our nerves and calm our minds. Help us God, instead of thinking about our fears and worries, help us to focus on your goodness, your faithfulness, your healing power, your overflowing resources, and your forgiving heart. Lord, take up residence within us and fill us with your peace. Show us what robbing us of it. We really want to know God and my Lord, so we can be specific in what we need to confess, and what we need to commit to and what we need to change. We open ourselves to you now. Lord. Teach us the secret of lasting peace. We thank You now for whatever it will take to help us receive the peace You have so generously offered us in Jesus' name Amen.

JOHN 14 VS 27 Peace I leave with you, my peace I give unto you; not as the world giveth, give I unto you. Let not your heart be troubled, neither let it be afraid.

*"Never speak from the reality of your circum-stances but speak from the reality of God's future perspective, very important."*

**Vivian Rodgers**

## CONFESSION

Our lives have been given a meaning. Therefore, we are impacting the lives of those around us positively. We are living meaningful lives. Thanks be to God almighty. We rejoice because it's given unto us to understand your word and hear your voice in our spirit. Thank you for the influence of your word in our life. The word of God is alive in us, we are making progress and profiting on every side. We are healthy, strong, excellent and vibrant. Our heart is a fertile ground and the word of God is producing great results in every area of our lives. We are one with the father; as so we are in this world, To God be the glory.

JOB 22 VS 18 to 28 Yet he filled their houses with

good things; but the counsel of the wicked is far from me. The righteous see it, and are glad and the innocent laugh them to scorn. Whereas our substance is not cut down, but the remnant of them the fire consumeth. Acquaint now thyself with him, and be at peace; thereby good shall come unto thee. Receive I pray thee, the law from his mouth, and lay up his words in thine heart. If thou return to the Almighty, thou shalt be built up, thou shalt put away iniquity far from thy tabernacle. Then shalt thou lay up gold as dust, and the gold of Ophir as the stones of the brooks. Yea, the Almighty shall be thy defence, and thou shalt have plenty of silver. For then shalt thou have thy delight in the Almighty, and shalt lift up thy face unto God. Thou shalt make thy prayer unto him, and he shall hear thee, and thou shalt pay thy vows. Thou shalt also decree a thing and it shall be established unto thee, and the light shall shine upon thy ways.

ISAIAH 61 VS 2 TO 7 To proclaim the acceptable year of the Lord, and the day of vengeance of our God; to comfort all that mourn; To appoint unto them that mourn in Zion, to give unto them beauty for ashes, the oil of joy for mourning, the garment of praise for the spirit of heaviness; that they might be called trees of righteousness, the planting of the Lord that he might he glorified. And they shall build the old wastes, they shall raise up the former desolation, and they shall repair the waste cities, the desolation of many generations. And strangers shall stand and feed your flocks and the sons of the alien shall be your ploughmen and your vinedressers. But ye shall be named the Priests of the Lord; men shall call you the Ministers of our God; ye shall eat the riches of the Gentiles and in their glory shall ye boast yourself. For your shame ye shall have double; and for your confusion they shall rejoice in their portion; therefore, in their land they shall possess the double; everlasting joy shall be unto them. Amen.

However, when you get acquainted with the word of God, it will help you to take responsibility for yourself. Moreover, you have to realise that Christianity is for talkers. Unfortunately, the word of God in your mouth is your assurance for a glorious, prosperous and successful future. Basically, that is why Jeremiah said that the word of God is like a fire and a hammer that breaketh the rock in pieces. Christianity is not religion but relationship. Christianity is everyday work by speaking the word in faith, by renewing your mind because your mind is in a battlefield. Obviously, that is why Satan is after your mind to destroy you.

JEREMIAH 23 VS 29 Is not my word as a fire? Saith the Lord and like a hammer. That breaketh the rock in pieces.

Jeremiah said he found the words of God and ate them, because the word of God is life, when you discover how to use it. However, that is why you have to study your Bible to help you in the time of trouble; unfortunately the Bible says the evil day is coming. Moreover, if you don't know the word in your spirit, how are you going to handle the trouble, when it knocks at your door. As a matter of fact, the word of God is God's light, which describes or defines your true identity and personality. Most likely, if you study or learn God's word, you will discover more about yourself and it will help you to locate yourself in Him. Hallelujah. However, as you develop the love of God from the word of God, you will be transformed to be a better person and you will make positive changes. Literally, do you know that the word of God is a lamp unto your feet and a light on your path? Eventually, it will help you develop confidence in yourself.

> 1 CORINTHIANS 2 VS 12 to 13 Now we have received, not the spirit of the world, but the spirit which is of God; that we might know the things that are freely given to us of God. Which things also we speak, not in the words which man's wisdom teacheth, but which the HOLY GHOST teacheth; comparing spirit things with spiritual.

> JEREMIAH 15 VS 16 Thy words were found, and I did eat them; and thy word was unto me the joy and rejoicing of my heart; for I am called by thy name LORD God of hosts.

> PSALM 119 VS 105 Thy word is a lamp unto my feet and a light unto my path.

GOD PROMISE TO YOU, IF YOU BELIEVE. GOD CAN NOT LIE.

> ISAIAH 65 VS 16 TO 24 That he who blesseth himself in the earth shall bless himself in the God of truth, and he that sweareth in the earth shall swear by the God of truth; because the former troubles are forgotten, and because they are hid from mine eyes. For behold I create new heavens and a new earth and the former shall not

be remembered nor come unto mine. But be you glad and rejoice forever in that which I create for behold create Jerusalem a rejoicing, and her people a joy. And I will rejoice in Jerusalem, and joy in my people; and the voice of weeping shall be no more heard in her nor the voice of crying. There shall be no more thence am infant of days, nor an old man that hath not filled his days for the child shall die a hundred years old shall be accursed. And they shall build house, and inhabit them; and they shall plant vineyards and eat the fruit of them. They shall not build and another inhabit; they shall not plant; and another eat; for as the days of a tree are the days of my people, and mine elect shall long enjoy the word of their hands. They shall not labour in vain nor bring forth for trouble; for they are the seed of the blessed of the LORD, and their offspring with them. And it shall come to pass, that before they call will answer, and while they are yet speaking will hear.

HEBREWS 6 VS 18 That by two immutable things, in which it was impossible for God to lie, we might have a strong consolation, who have fled refuge to hold upon the hope set before us. Which hope we have as an anchor of the soul, both sure and steadfast, and which entereth into that within the veil;

Actually, when your mind is renewed and you have a good mindset, look at what God promise us, your God cannot lie. And the sons of strangers shall build up thy walls, and their Kings shall minister unto thee; for in my wrath I smote thee, but in my favour have I had mercy on thee. Therefore, thy gates shall be open continually; they shall not be shut day nor night; that men may bring unto thee the forces of the Gentiles, and that their Kings may be brought. For the nation and Kingdom that will not serve thee shall perish; yea, those nations shall be utterly wasted. The glory of Lebanon shall come unto thee, the fir tree, the pine tree and the box together; to beautify the place of my sanctuary; and I will make the place of my feet glorious. The sons of them that afflicted thee shall come bending unto thee; and all they that despised thee shall bow themselves down at the soles of thy feet; and they shall call thee, the city of the Lord, The Zion of the Holy One of Israel, whereas thou hast been forsaken and hatreds that no man went through thee, I will make thee an eternal excellency, a joy of many generations. Amen. Believe and trust God He cannot lie. **[ISAIAH 60 VS 10 TO 14]**

## CONFESSION

O God, help us to understand your ways and not to walk in our own integrity. Help us to trust in the Lord with all our heart and not to lean on our own understanding, that in all our ways we will acknowledge you and you will direct our paths. My Lord and our God, we thank you for giving us the ability to speak words of life and words that carry the power to alter our condition and destiny for good, we are grateful to know that you delight in us and we become your pleasure. Glory be to God almighty.

Obviously, renew your mind means your mindset to change because many people are stagnant with the wrong mindset. That leads them to question God or doubt God's promise. Moreover, because of their wrong mindset, they become a victim of going from one church to another. Usually, they never enjoy God's benefit because the word of God is not in their life. However, when you keep the word in your heart and in your mouth day and night, it will produce a new mindset of victory, success and advantage. Moreover, make sure you keep pondering, muttering and shouting the word. Basically, for you to have a good mindset, you have to place what is conducive where you can shut your mind down and talk your spirit up with the word of God in your spirit. As a matter of fact, make sure you practise and you will have a renewed mindset. Actually, you will notice that you talk differently and your friends will notice that there is something unique about you; most of them will not like you again as before because they feel that you are now full of yourself. Don't take any notice of them, because we are running a heavenly race. Beloved, keep word in your mouth and you will come back with a testimony. Moreover, meditate on the word of God to help you build up and enable you to develop spiritual and mental attitudes that are consistent with God's will and purpose for your life. Moreover, to be word empty is risky, because the word of God is quick, and powerful, and sharper than any two-edged sword, piercing even in the dividing asunder of soul and spirit, and of the joints and marrow and is a discerner of the thoughts and intents of the heart.

> JOB 36 VS 5 to 6 Behold, God is mighty, and despiseth not any; he is mighty in strength and wisdom. He preserveth not the life of the wicked; but giveth right to the poor; He with draweth not his eyes from the righteous; but with Kings are they on the throne; yea he doth establish them for ever, and they are exalted.

Moreover, our mind is who we are, be honest see your character and see how you behave, that shows you. Your mind controls you. Basically, you must take care and guard it against the corrupting influences that are everywhere in our world. However, when you engage your mind, you cannot be trapped in any situation. Actually, you have to shrewdly discern the subtle voices that are constantly presenting seemingly appealing ideologies. Which are, in fact, opposed to God. Obviously, you have to train yourselves, through the scriptures, to discern good from bad. Indeed, you have to guard your hearts and minds through prayer and upright thoughts. Moreover, Apostle Paul gave us assurance that God will guard our hearts and minds when we surrender everything to Him in prayer.

PHILIPPIANS 4 VS 6 be careful for nothing; but in everything by prayer and supplication with thanksgiving, let your request be made known unto God.

ISAIAH 11 VS 2 to 4 And the spirit of the Lord shall rest upon him, the spirit of wisdom and understanding, the spirit of counsel and might, the spirit of knowledge and of the fear of the Lord. And shall make him of quick under-standing in the fear of the Lord; and he shall not judge after the sight of his eyes, neither reprove after the hearing of his ears.

JOB 34 VS 29 When he giveth quietness, who then can make trouble? And when he hideth his face; who then can behold him?

*"You need the right people with you, not the best people."*

**Jack Ma**

Literally, there is another way we can renew our minds, moreover for our life transformed – it is to go to the very root of our problems we are facing. Obviously, until we get in to the issue, we are not really renewing our minds at all. Actually, that is the fact because the choices you make today will determine your positions tomorrow. Moreover, we have to renew our minds because our minds are under attack every day. However, the mind is a fascinating creation as this is the place where realty begins. Although the solution to every problem you face is contained in scripture. Moreover, to be wise you must study it, to be strong in faith you must believe it. To be successful in life you must practice it because faith is the secret of your success. Once you understand that, your struggle will begin to make sense. However, when your mind is renewed, confidence and quietness shall be your strength. Actually, as you study God's word you will begin to experience the mind-renewing and life-changing power he has deposited within you. Christ is able to do immeasurably more than all we ask or imagine according to his power that is working in us. Their friend starts to draw on the power today. Do you know what's in you? Obviously, there are words in the Bible that have so much life and power in them and are stronger than any therapy. God can give you a word that goes back into your past and heals your yesterday, secures your today, and anchors your tomorrow. Glory be to God. Moreover, that is why

Satan clutters your life with so much junk that you don't have time for God's word. Most likely Satan knows if we unmask him and reveal the God potential that's lying dormant within you; you will never compromise in things of God. Hallelujah.

> ISAIAH 30 VS 15 For thus saith the Lord God, the Holy One of Israel; In returning and rest shall ye be saved; in quietness and in confidence shall be your strength. And ye would not.

> ISAIAH 30 VS 18 to 21 And therefore will the LORD wait that he may be gracious unto you and therefore will he be exalted he may have mercy upon you; for the Lord is God of judgment; blessed are all they that wait for him. For the people shall dwell in Zion at Jerusalem; thou shalt weep no more; he will be very gracious unto thee at the voice of thy cry; when he shall hear it, he will answer thee. And though the Lord give you the bread of adversity, and the water of affliction, yet shall not thy teachers be removed into a corner anymore, but thine eyes shall see thy teacher. And thine ears shall hear a word behind thee, saying, This is the way, walk ye in it, when ye turn to the right hand, and when you turn to the left.

> ISAIAH 26 VS 3 to 4 Thou wilt keep him in perfect peace whose mind is stayed thee; because he trusteth in thee. Trust ye in the LORD for ever; for in the LORD JEHOVAH is everlasting strength;

Basically, before Jeremiah rose to the prominence as a

prophet God told him; before I formed you in the womb I knew you. Your parents didn't get the first look at you, God did. Nothing about you surprises him. Moreover, in spite of what you have been through, he hasn't changed his mind about who you are or what you are destined to become before you were born. Almighty God set you apart, stop looking for acceptance in the places where you don't belong. You are on a mission for God. That's why the enemy has tried so hard to take you out. Once you understand that, your struggles will begin to make sense. However, when you develop time to study God's word it will enable you to understand the awesomeness of the mind-renewing, thirst-quenching, life-changing potential that was deposited within you from before the foundation of the world. Actually, any time you face opposition, know that you have a great position, because Satan will never fight you if you have nothing to offer. Moreover, don't allow what won't matter tomorrow trouble your today. Literally, if you can take advantage of these words, the opinion of people will not determine where you will end up, but become irrelevant and don't count. As a matter of fact, when people don't know your story, they will understand your joy because they haven't been where you are and what you have been through in life.

> ECCLESIASTES 7 VS 11 to 12 Wisdom is good with an inheritance and by it there is profit to them that see the sun. For wisdom is a defence, and money is a defence but the excellency of knowledge is, that wisdom giveth life to them that have it.

Basically, I'm a living testimony because I never knew I would be a publisher. In the midst of my challenges I started discovering my potential and who I am, by renewing my mind in that difficult time. Literally when you keep on renewing your mind, it will help to discover God's love over your life and your purpose. Hallelujah. Beloved, do you know you are God's glory. You are God's special. You are God's expression. You are God's solution and it is working in you. You are God's wisdom and it is working over you, that is why you renew your mind always. Obviously, it doesn't matter what you are going through because you are blessed to be a blessing. Moreover, a wise woman is the one that recognizes that life is not meant to be lived for self but that life was designed by the Creator to help other people; and to make a definite change in one's generation.

> PSALM 37 VS 7 to 9 Rest in the Lord and wait patiently for him; fret not thyself because of him who prospereth in his way because of the man who bringeth wicked devices to pass. Cease from anger; and forsake wrath not thyself in any wise to do evil. For evildoers shall be cut off; but those that wait upon the Lord they shall inherit the earth.

> JEREMIAH 1 VS 5 Before I formed thee in the belly I knew thee; and before thou camest forth out of the womb I sanctified thee, and I ordained thee a prophet unto the nations.

> PHILIPPIANS 4 VS 13 I can do all things through Christ which strengtheneth me.

> PSALM 16 VS 5 to 11 The Lord is the portion of mine inheritance and of my cup thou maintainest my lot. The lines are fallen unto me in pleasant places; yea, I have a goodly heritage. I will bless

the Lord, who hath given me counsel; my reins also instruct me in the night seasons. I have set the Lord always before me; because he is at my right hand, I shall not be moved. Therefore, my heart is glad and my glory rejoice; my flesh also shall rest in hope. For thou wilt not leave my soul in hell; neither wilt thou suffer thine Holy One to see corruption. Thou wilt shew me the path of life; in thy presence is fulness of joy; at thy right hand there are pleasures for evermore.

Actually, when you renew your mind, all it takes is one daring decision, that's all it even takes. Moreover, when you move, God will move on your behalf, and if you don't move you will always wonder; what if? Our longest regrets are caused by our inaction. However, that is why we have to renew our mind and know what we want in our life. Basically, before you leave this earth, endeavour to give to others what God has entrusted in you. As a matter of fact, many Christians never live their life; instead, they are living other people's dreams. Moreover, you see them going from one church to another, and at the end they never achieve anything in their life. Although, as you renew your mindset, you will discover what God entrusted to you because it is inside you. Fortunately, when you doubt God, you disappoint Him. Because He deserves better. You know God cannot lie. Therefore, you must seek to strengthen your faith, because faith honours God and God honours faith. Beloved, with God on your side, you can say; whatever I'm afraid I will trust in you. However, that will happen when you know who you are and renew your mindset. Most likely the way you think determines the way you feel. Moreover, when your feeling becomes strong enough, that will determine the way you act. Actually, the person who says *cannot do it*, and the person who says *can do it*, are both right. Most of the time you set yourself up to be defeated by what you are saying. Obviously, your words reinforce either your right or wrong belief system.

> PSALM 46 VS 1 God is our refuge and strength, a very present help in trouble.

> PROVERB 18 VS 21 Death and life are in the power of the tongue; and they that love it shall eat the fruit therefore.

> ECCLESIASTES 10 VS 10 If the iron be blunt, and he do not whet the edge, then much he put to more strength; but wisdom is profitable to direct.

> MARK 11 VS 24 Therefore say unto you, what things soever ye desire, when ye pray believe that ye receive them, and ye shall have them.

> MARK 9 VS 23 Jesus said unto him, If thou canst believe, all things are possible to him that believeth.

Moreover, there are three things in First Peter, God reminds us to have a clear mind and self-control. Why? Because a clear mind is essential to self-control. God gave us the power to choose our thoughts, that is why Roman twelve verse two tells you to be transformed by renewing your mind. However, when your self-control is being tested, you need to fill your mind with the promises of God, here's one; when you are tempted, he will also provide a way out so that you can stand up under the temptation.

Actually, you have to believe God when He says there's a way out for you. Paul writes: my grace is sufficient for you, for my power is made perfect in weakness.

> 1 CORINTHIANS 10 VS 13 There hath no temptation taken you but such as is common man but GOD IS FAITHFUL, WHO WILL NOT SUFFER YOU TO BE TEMPTED ABOVE THAT YE ARE ABLE; BUT WILL WITH THE TEMPTATION ALSO MAKE A WAY TO ESCAPE, THAT YE MAY BE ABLE TO BEAR IT.

> ISAIAH 14 VS 24 The Lord of hosts hath sworn saying, surely as I have thought, so shall it come to pass; and as I have purpose, so shall it stand. Hallelujah.

> PSALM 124 VS 6 to 8 Blessed be the Lord, who hath not given us as prey to their teeth. Our soul is escaped as a bird out of the snare of the fowlers; the snare is broken, and we are escaped. Our help is the name of The Lord, who made heaven and earth.

However, when God said that his grace is sufficient for you, that mean can change and you can be different. Stop setting yourself up for failure by constantly criticising yourself. Don't allow *am not qualified* into your life. Actually, for you to have a bad attitude doesn't work for you or anyone else. Obviously, God cannot send us in any situation alone, He always go head of us, He stands beside us, He walks behind us. Literally, whatever situation you find yourself in, be confident to know that He is there with you. He said: I never leave you nor forsake you. He cannot lie.

HEBREWS 13 VS 5 to 6 Let your conversation be without covetousness; and be content with such things as ye have; for he hath said I will never leave thee, nor forsake thee. So that we may boldly say, The Lord is my helper; and I will not fear what man shall do unto me. Hallelujah.

HEBREWS 6 VS 18 That by two immutable things, in which it was impossible for God to lie, we might have a strong consolation, who have fled for refuge to lay hold upon the home set before us,

PSALM 61 VS 1 to 4 Hear my cry O God; attend unto my prayer; From the end of the earth will I cry unto thee, when my heart is overwhelmed lead me to the rock that is higher than I. For thou have been a shelter for me and a strong tower from the enemy. I will abide in thy tabernacle for ever; I will trust in the cover of thy wings. Selah.

MATTHEW 28 VS 18 to 20 And Jesus came and spake unto them, saying. All power is given unto me in heaven and earth. Go ye therefore, and teach all nations, baptizing them in the name of the Father, and of the Son, and of the Holy Ghost; Teaching them to observe all things whatsoever I have commanded you; and lo, I am with you always, even unto the end of the world, Amen.

Basically, your mind is powerful enough to pick anything, because your mind is where you think good and bad. Obviously, you have to control your mind by not using negative words because your mind is more than mere imagination; your mind is a mental picture with constructions or destructive capabilities. However, with your mind you can create things, as a matter of fact do you know that the mental construction of your mind is based on your imagination. Most likely it has the power to keep you in bondage or to liberate you, to be a better person. Actually, that is why you have to protect your mind by renewing it day by day. Moreover, you have to guard your heart and mind seriously because there are lots of TV programmes, movies, music and magazines that you won't watch if you want to be saturated and empowered by the Holy Spirit. Literally, you can guard your hearts and minds through the knowledge of God's word. Basically, you should not feed your minds with words that promote sinful thoughts. Moreover, God cannot stop your thinking be it good or bad; that is why you have to think positively to gain positive results. Obviously, God never says: *let us pray together*; instead, He says: *come let us reason together*. That means your mind is needed, iron sharpening iron. In other words, you are to pursue hard after God and put aside sinful thoughts with godly pursuits and mindsets. As a matter of fact, that's the principle of replacement. If you're tempted to hate somebody, you replace those hateful thoughts with godly actions. Literally, learn to be good to them, speak well of them and pray for them, and the peace of God, which passeth all understanding, shall keep your hearts and minds through Christ Jesus, Moreover, be a Prayerful person, because that is the key; but working hard too is the key. Hard work will take you places in life. Actually, it will raise you to stand before Kings and great people. Promotion comes with hard work, Basically, it is impossible to be diligent and work hard and remain poor. Success will come to the woman who works hard for it. Can I be honest with you? Any life that is not spending time doing what he or she was created to do, is wasting time because time waits for nobody. Apostle Paul said: be careful for nothing; but in everything by prayer and supplication with thanksgiving, let your requests be made known unto God.

> DANIEL 12 VS 2 to 3 And many of them that sleep in the dust the earth shall awake, some to everlasting contempt. And they that be wise shall shine as the brightness of the firmament; and they that turn many to righteousness as the stars for ever and ever.

> ECCLESIASTES 4 VS 5 TO 6 The fool foldeth his hands together, and eateth his own flesh. Better is an handful with quietness. Than both the hands full with travail and vexation of spirit.

> ECCLESIASTES 3 VS 1 TO 4 To everything there is a season, and a time to every purpose under the heaven; A time to be born, and a time to die; a time to plant, and a time to pluck up that which is planted; A time to kill, and a time to heal; a time to break down, and a time to build up; A time to weep, and a time to laugh; a time to mourn, and a time to dance;

> PROVERBS 30 VS 24 TO 25 There be four things which are little upon the earth, but they are exceeding wise; The ants are a people not strong, yet they prepare their meat in the summer.

> PROVERBS 18 VS 15 TO 16 The heart of the prudent getteth knowledge and the ear of the wise seeketh knowledge. A man's gift maketh

room for him, and bringeth him before great men.

PHILIPPIANS 4 VS 4 TO 7 Rejoice in the Lord always; and again, I says, Rejoice. Let your moderation be known unto all men. The Lord is at hand. Be careful for nothing; but in everything by prayer and supplication with thanksgiving, let your requests be made known unto God. And the peace of God which passeth all understanding, shall keep your hearts and minds through Christ Jesus.

Although renewing your mind is an important part of living a successful life. Moreover, there are few principles that will help you better understand the concept of *renew your mind*. First, understand that God is not willing that any should perish. Not only is it His will for you to be saved but it is also His will for you to be free so you can know what is that good and acceptable and perfect will of God for your life. However, you need to know that God reveals his will for mankind through his word. In fact, as you study and put your trust in God you will discover your purpose in life. Basically, as you renew your mind, there is no obstacle too hard for you; moreover, when you stay focused, you will achieve your goal. As you keep on renewing your mind, it will enable you to see any challenges as opportunities because an opportunity missed you can't get back. Categorically, if you keep on renewing your mind and do the right thing you will discover the greatness that is you.

PHILIPPIANS 4 VS 7 And the peace of God, which passeth all understanding, shall keep your hearts and minds through Christ Jesus.

Basically, there is power in a quiet mind, because our creative mind is activated during time of mental quietness. John Maxwell gave his final thoughts by saying: "If you are not doing something with your life, it doesn't matter how long it is."

If you are doing something with your life. it doesn't matter how long it is. Life does not come of years. Although *renew your mind* requires faith when acting on the word of God. As you renew your mind, you need peace which transcends *understanding my nerves* and *calm your mind*. Moreover, instead of thinking about your fears and worries, Lord, help us to stay focussed on your goodness, mercy, faithfulness, your healing power, your overflowing resources, and your forgiving heart over us. Hallelujah. My Lord and my God, take up residence within us and fill us with your peace, Moreover, show us what's robbing us of it. My God, we really want to know so we can know the specific in what we need to confess, and what we need to commit to and what we need to change. We open our self to you now Lord. Teach us the secret of lasting peace Lord which you have so generously offered to us., we thank you now for whatever it will take to help us receive the peace. Your words say: "Let the peace of Christ rule in your hearts."

God promises, thus saith the Lord, thy redeemer, and he that formed thee from thee from the womb. I am the Lord that maketh all things; that stretcheth forth the heavens alone; that spreadeth abroad the earth by myself; That frustrateth the tokens of the liars, and maketh diviners mad; that turneth wise men backward, and maketh their knowledge foolish; That confirmeth the word of his servant, and performeth the counsel of his messenger; that saith to Jerusalem, thou shalt be inhabited, and to the cities of Judah, Ye shall be built and I will raise up the decayed places thereof. Same applicable to you, what he said to one say it to all. If you believe all things are possible to them that believe, God cannot lie. **[ISAIAH 44 VS 24 to 26]**

# LET US PRAY

O Lord and my God, today we want to be ruled by your peace, instead of your fears and worries, so we give all our concerns to you, trusting you to work them out for our good and your glory. Our God shall wipe away all tears from our eyes; and there shall be no more death, neither shall there be any more pain; for the former things are passed away. May God bless us with what we work for. Grant us with what we hope for. Moreover, surprise us with what you have not asked for. In Jesus name we pray. Amen.

> ISAIAH 62 VS 1 to 5 For Zion's sake will I not hold my peace, and for Jerusalem's sake I will not rest, until the righteousness thereof go forth as brightness, and the salvation thereof as a lamp that burneth. And the Gentiles shall see thy righteousness, and all Kings thy glory and thou shalt be called by a new name, which the mouth of the Lord shall name. Thou shalt also be a crown of glory in the hand of the Lord, and a royal diadem in the hand of God. Thou shalt no more be termed. Forsaken neither shall thy land any more be termed Desolate; but thy shalt be called Hephzibah, and thy land Beulah; for the Lord delighteth in thee, and thy land shall be married. For as a young man marrieth a virgin, so shall thy sons marry thee and as the bride-

groom rejoice over the bride, so shall thy God rejoice over thee.

*"Never speak from the reality of your circumstances but speak from the reality of God's future perspective. Very important."*

**Vivian Rodgers**

Basically, as Christians we have to renew our minds every day, by speaking the word of God in our spirit. Obviously, you have to know that our weapons of our warfare are not carnal but pulling down the strongholds. How will you do that? By renewing your mind because Satan is after your destiny. Categorically that is why Satan is attracting your mind. However, if you fall by his lies, eventually you will start seeing defeat, fear, and failure. As a matter fact, you start imagining what is going to happen to you. The devil is a liar. That is why God said cast down and bring it into captivity in to God's obedience. Beloved we are at war in this world. Basically, you know God makes everything work out according to his plan. Does that mean Paul understood every detail of God's plan? O no but when he didn't understand, he trusted the planner and kept moving. Literally, that's where Paul's peace, Joy, and contentment came from. Obviously, the same is applicable to you. The almighty God withholds no good thing from those who do what is perfect in his sight. Glory be to God.

PSALM 84 VS 11 to 12 For the Lord God is a sun and shield; the Lord will give grace and glory; no good thing will he withhold from them that walk uprightly. Lord of hosts, blessed is the man that trusteth in thee. God cannot lie, trust Him.

# CONFESSION

My Lord, thank you for letting me know that I have to protect my mind, by not speaking any negative words, by taking control of my mind and renewing it day by day. Moreover, if I renew my mind, it will transform me from glory to glory. Amen.

EPHESIANS 6 VS 10 TO 19 Finally; my brethren, be strong in the Lord, and in the power of his might. Put on the whole armour of God, that ye may be able to stand against the wiles of the devil. For we wrestle not against flesh and blood but against principalities, against power, against the rulers of the darkness of this world, against spiritual wickedness in high places. Wherefore take unto you the whole armour of God, that ye may be able to withstand unto the evil day, and having done all, to stand. Stand therefore, have your loins girded about with truth, and having on the breastplate of righteousness; And your feet shod with the preparation of the gospel of peace; Above all, taking the shield of faith, wherewith ye shall be able to quench all the fiery darts of the wicked. And take the helmet of salvation, and the sword of the Spirit, which is the word of God. Praying always with all prayer and supplication in the Spirit, and for me, that utterance may open my mouth boldly, to make known the mystery of the gospel, watching thereunto with all perseverance and supplication for all saints. One motivational speaker by the name Zig Ziglar said: what you picture in your mind, your mind will go to work to accomplish. However, when you change your pictures, you automatically change your performance. Glory be to God. However, you know that each person is the principal factor that determines success in their life, that is way you have to think right, and stop thinking problems and stop exaggerating things because that will make you develop a spirit of fear. Moreover, fear opens doors for failure. Actually, you know fear tolerated is faith contaminated. Moreover, if you cannot transform your mind, it cannot give you wealth because a mind renewed is prosperity giving. Hallelujah.

COLOSSIANS 3 VS 15 to 16 And let the peace of God rule in your hearts, to which also ye are called in one body; and be ye thankful. Let the word of Christ dwell in you richly in all wisdom; teaching and admonishing one another in psalms and hymns and spiritual songs, singing with grace in your hearts to the Lord.

*"Take risks, if you win you be happy and if you lose you will be wiser."*

**Jason Statham**

# CONFESSION

O God, help us to understand your ways and not to walk in our own integrity. Help us to trust in the Lord with all our heart and not to lean on our own understanding. Moreover, in all our ways we will acknowledge you and you will direct your path. Amen.

God promises, thus saith the Lord that made thee, and formed thee from the womb, which will help thee; Fear not, O Jacob, my servant; and thou, Jeshurun, whom I has chosen. For I will pour water upon him that is thirsty, and floods upon the dry ground will pour my spirit upon thy seed, and my blessing upon thine offspring; And they shall spring up as among the grass, as willows by the water courses. The same is applicable to you if you believe and trust God with his word and promises. God is a covenant keeper and he cannot be a liar. **[ISAIAH 44 VS 2 TO 4.]**

> 1 CORINTHIANS 9 VS 10 Or saith he it altogether for our sakes? For our sakes, no doubt, this is written; that he that ploweth should plow in hope; and that he that thresheth in hope should be partaker of his hope. Amen.

Obviously, as believers we must go through life with consciousness of our spiritual position at all times, because often we may get into battle with our enemies and we lose sight of our heavenly position and the enemy pulls us down to their level. However, you mustn't get into flesh or allow yourselves to fall into their traps. Basically, it will become harder to fight them. Actually, with consistent awareness of our spiritual authority, eventually you will override the enemy's attacks and subdue him. Literally, that's why you have to know the word of God for yourself, it will enable you to stay focussed and not be a victim. Moreover, it will minimize you from going to church to church. Actually, if only you can learn how to close the door in your house and pray, the almighty God will hear you because He never changes; He is a faithful God who said call on me in time of troubles and I will answer you, show you the things you knew not. God cannot lie. His words are yes and amen. Hallelujah. He said call on me, not call on man or woman. And he said again looking on to Jesus. He is almighty God who never fails and He is not a respecter of anybody and He is not God of partiality. Moreover, if he can answer Esther the Queen and her family, He will answer you; just trust God and his words. Moreover, to be word empty is risky so know the word of God for yourself.

HEBREW 12 VS 2 Looking unto Jesus the author and finisher of our faith; Who for the Joy that was set before him endured the cross despising the shame and is set down at the right hand of the throne of God.

JEREMIAH 33 VS 3 Call unto me, and I will answer thee, and shew thee great and mighty things, which thou knowest not.

PSALM 55 VS 16 TO 17 As for me will call upon God; and the Lord shall save me. Evening and morning; and at noon will I pray and cry aloud and he shall hear my voice. He hath delivered my soul in peace from the battle that was against me; for there were many with me.

1 CHRONICLES 15 VS 7 Be ye strong therefore, and let not your hands be weak; for your work shall be rewarded. Amen.

PSALM 138 VS 7 TO 8 Though I walk in the midst of trouble, thou will revive me; Thou shalt stretch forth thine hand against the wrath of mine enemies, and thy right hand shall save me. The Lord will perfect that which concerneth me; thy mercy Lord, endured for ever; forsake not the works of thine own hands. Unfortunately, it is crucial you renew your mind often, it will enable to develop a new mindset.

2 CORINTHIANS 1 VS 20 For all the promises of God in him are yea and in him, Amen unto the glory of God by us.

# LET US PRAY

My God, My Lord. We thank you for your goodness and mercy over us. We thank you for your care and love you show us, even in the darkest hour you are always there for us. My God we are grateful. My God cause us to hear thy loving kindness in the morning; for in thee do we trust. O Lord cause us to know the way where we should walk; for we lift up our soul unto you. Deliver us from our enemies, we flee unto thee to hide us. My Lord, teach us to do your will, for you are our God. Your spirit is good, lead us into the land of uprightness. My Father and Lord, quicken us O Lord for your name's sake, bring our life out of trouble in Jesus' name we pray. My God and my God as we hold unto the righteousness of our Lord Jesus Christ. Please do not permit us to be moved by the scheming of the evil doers in the mighty name of Jesus. May we be truly blessed to become blessings to others and as we do, may we be bountifully rewarded here on the earth and beyond in the Mighty name of Jesus name. Amen.

PSALM 67 VS 1 to 7] God be merciful unto us, and bless us; and cause his face to shine upon us. That thy way may be known upon earth, thy saving health among all nations. Let the people praise thee, O God let all the people praise thee. O let all nations be glad and sing for joy thou shalt judge the people righteously, and govern the nations upon earth. Let the people praise thee. O God let all the people praise thee. Then shall the earth yield her increases and God, even our own God, shall bless us. God shall bless us; and all the ends of the earth shall fear him. Amen.

GALATIANS 6 VS 9 And let us not be weary in well doing; for in due season, we shall reap. If we faint not. Amen.

ISAIAH 61 VS 1 to 7 The spirit of God is up me; because the Lord hath anointed me to preach good tidings unto the meek; he hath sent me to bind up the broken-hearted to proclaim liberty to the captives, and opening of the captives, and the opening of the prison to them that are bound; To proclaim the acceptable year of the Lord ;and the day of vengeance of our God to comfort all that mourn; To appoint unto them that mourn in Zion. to give unto them beauty for ashes, the oil of joy for mourning, garment of praise spirit of heaviness; that they might be called trees of righteousness, the planting of the Lord, that he might be glorified. And they shall build the old wastes, they shall raise up the former desolations, and they shall repair the waste cities the desolations of many generations. And strangers shall stand and feed your flocks, and the sons of the alien shall be your plowmen and your vinedressers. But ye shall be named the priests of the Lord men shall call you the Ministers of our God; ye shall eat the riches of the Gentiles and in their glory shall ye boast yourselves. For your shame ye shall have double; and for confusion they shall rejoice in their portion; therefore, in their land they shall possess double; everlasting joy shall be unto them.

# CONFESSION

Lord. We thank you for giving us the ability to speak words of life and words that carry the power to alter our condition and destiny for good. We are grateful to know that you delight in us and we become your pleasure. Amen.

Actually, as Christians we have to guard our hearts because Satan will come and whisper to us that God's promise is not true. Obviously, most of the time he will make you feel bad about yourself. However, if your mind is not renewed, Satan will make you doubt God. As a matter of fact, that's why you have to read your Bible always. For instance, look at Adam and Eve, how Satan made them question God's promise, even disobey God's instruction, by asking Eve if it was true that God told her you eat of; if you eat fruit of this tree in the garden, you shall surely die? Basically, that is why you have to guard your heart because Satan is going to act like a lion but he is a dog seeking who he will deceive. He is a liar and a thief. Moreover, the flow of the mind and thinking determines the flow of the miraculous.

> JOHN 1 VS 10 The thief cometh not but for to steal and to kill and to destroy; I am come that they might have life and that they might have it more abundantly.

> ISAIAH 65 VS 20 TO 24 There shall be no more thence am infant of days, nor an old man that hath not filled his days for the child shall die a hundred years old shall be accursed. And they shall build house, and inhabit them; and they shall plant vineyards and eat the fruit of them.

They shall not build and another inhabit; they shall not plant; and another eat; for as the days of a tree are the days of my people, and mine elect shall long enjoy the word of their hands. They shall not labour in vain nor bring forth for trouble; for they are the seed of the blessed of the LORD, and their offspring with them. And it shall come to pass, that before they call will answer, and while they are yet speaking will hear.

JUDE 1 VS 24 Now unto him that is able to keep you from falling and to present you faultless before the presence of his glory with exceeding Joy. To the only wise God our Saviour be glory and majesty, dominion and power; both now and ever. Amen.

JOHN 8 VS 44 Ye are of your father the devil and the lusts of your father ye will do. He was a murderer from the beginning and abode not in the truth because there is no truth in him. When he speaketh a lie he speaketh of his own; for he is a liar; and the father of it.

GENESIS 3 VS 1 TO 2  Now the serpent was more subtle than any beast of the field which the Lord God had made. And he said unto the woman, Yea hath God said Ye shall not eat of every tree of the garden. And the woman said unto the serpent. We may eat of the fruit of the trees of the garden. But of the fruit of the tree which is in the midst of the garden, God hath said, ye shall not eat of it, neither shall ye touch it. Lest ye die.

Literally renew your mind with scripture is an important ad tool for God's will being done in your life. Obviously when your mind is renewed it will enable you to change the way you think. Moreover, you will become creative because your mind is open to new things. You will develop the peace that passeth understanding, as the scripture said. God said cast thy body upon the Lord and he shall sustain thee; he shall never suffer the righteous to be moved. Honestly when your mind is renewed you will be far from stagnation because your mind is on another level. Hallelujah.

> COLOSSIANS 33 VS 14 TO 16 And above all these things put on charity; which is the bond of perfectness. And let the peace of God rule in your heart to the which also ye are called in one body; and be ye thankful. Let the word of Christ dwell in you richly in all wisdom; teaching and admonishing one another in psalms and hymns and spiritual songs; singing with grace in your hearts to the Lord. And whatsoever ye do in word or deed do all in the name of the Lord Jesus giving thanks to God and the Father by him. Glory be to God.

> PSALM 37 VS 3 TO 5 Trust in the Lord and do good; so shalt thou dwell in the land and verily thou shalt be fed. Delight thyself also in the Lord; and he shall give thee the desires of thine heart. Commit thy way unto the Lord; trust also in him and he shall bring it to pass.

> PHILIPPIANS 4 VS 7 And the peace of God which passeth all understanding; shall keep your

hearts and minds through Christ Jesus. Amen.

LUKE 10 VS 21 In that hour Jesus rejoiced in spirit and said thank thee; O Father Lord of heaven and earth. That thou hast hid these things from the wise and prudent; and hast revealed them unto babes; ever so. Father; for so it seemed good in thy sight.

## WHO I AM, BE YOURSELF?
You are express image of the father.
You are the outshining of his glory.
You are God's perfection beauty
You are the fullness of God almighty.
You are totality of God almighty. Hallelujah.

You are a chosen generation, a Royal priesthood, an Holy nation, a Peculiar people, that ye should shew forth the praise of him who hath called you out of darkness into his marvellous light. Glory be to God almighty.

EXODUS 15 VS 11 Who is like unto thee O Lord among the gods? Who is like thee glorious in holiness fearful in praises doing wonders? Hallelujah.

You are complete in Him. And your life is hiding in Christ in God.

COLOSSIANS 3 VS 1 TO 4 If ye then be risen with Christ seek those things which are above where Christ sitteth on the right hand of God. Set your affection on things above not on things on the earth. For ye are dead and your life is hid with Christ in God. When Christ who is our life shall appear; then shall ye also appear with him in glory. Hallelujah.

You are God's solution with you nothing is made that was made because you are his workmanship created in Christ Jesus unto his good works. Glory be to God almighty.

> ZEPHANIAH 3 VS 19 TO 20 Behold at that time I will undo all that afflict thee; and I will save her that halteth and I will get them praise and fame in every land where they have been put to shame. At that time will I bring you again even in the time that I gather you; for I will make you a name and a praise among all people of the earth when I turn back your captivity before your eyes saith the LORD. Hallelujah.

You are God's masterpiece. Hallelujah.

> EPHESIANS 2 VS 8 TO 10 For by grace are ye saved through faith; and that not of yourself; it is the gift of God; Not of works lest any man should boast. For we are his workmanship created in Christ Jesus unto good works which God hath before ordained that we should walk in them.

> 1 PETER 2 VS 21 TO 22 For even hereunto were ye called; because Christ also suffered for us, leaving Christ also suffered for us, leaving us an example, that ye should follow his steps; who did no sin, neither was guile found in his mouth.

# BE YOURSELF

*Be yourself* definition is: for you to behave in a natural way, rather than trying to be somebody else However, be yourself does not mean you are selfish or you don't care about others, Be yourself means you like who you are.

Moreover, don't worry about what people think about you. Obviously respect their opinion of others but don't let them push you in a different direction if you don't agree with them. Actually, when you make up your mind to be yourself, you notice that you carry yourself in another way, because you want to portray the new you. Obviously, some people may feel you are weird, that's okay. That is their own opinion. Just appreciate who you are, because everybody has their own uniqueness. Literally, who you are when you are alone by yourself, when no one is watching you, that's the real you. How motivated are you when nobody encourages you? Actually, you have to love who you are, that's all that matters. Moreover, don't allow anybody to change who you are. People will judge you, regardless of what you know or what you don't know. Just be yourself and make the best out of life, because we only come once; it is only James Bond that comes twice. However never compare yourself to others, just be yourself. Obviously, be positive about what you like and dislike. Moreover, work out what interests you. Actually the only way you can understand who you are, is to think about what you like and what you dislike when you are alone. That will enable you to know the real you. Hallelujah.

Moreover, there is one man call Jabez. The mother called him Jabez because she bore him without sorrow. As a matter of fact, when he grew up, he decided to be himself, not minding what the mother thought about him. Jabez was more honourable than his brethren but the mother didn't know who he was even though she was his mother. However, Jabez had another mindset of himself. Jabez called on God of Israel, saying oh that thou wouldest bless me indeed and enlarge my coast and that thine hand might be with me and that thou wouldest keep me from evil. Moreover, that it may not grieve me. Obviously, God granted him that which he requested. Hallelujah. Jabez knew that he had something that nobody would take away from him. That is why he called upon his God of Israel, the God who sees from beginning to the end. Most likely nobody knows you like you know yourself. Not even your parents. Actually, that is why you have to be yourself not minding what people think about you.

> 1 CHRONICLES 4 VS 9 TO 10 And Jabez was more honourable than his brethren and his mother called his name Jabez, saying, because I bare him with sorrow. And Jabez called on the God of Israel, saying, oh that thou wouldest bless me indeed and enlarge my coast, and that thine hand might be with me, and that thou wouldest keep me from evil, that it may not grieve me! And God granted him that which he requested.

> PSALM 139 VS 14 TO 15 will praise thee; for I am fearfully and wonderfully made; marvellous are thy works; and that my soul knoweth right well. My substance was not hid from thee, when I was made in secret and curiously wrought in the lowest parts of the earth.

Basically, not only are we wonderfully made but because of Christ's death on the cross, we can also be wonderfully restored to a relationship with God. Moreover, when you are in Christ, you are a new creation. All this is from God, who reconciled us to Himself through Christ. If anyone is in Christ, he is a new creation. Glory be to God.

> 2 CORINTHIAN 5 VS 17 TO 18 Therefore if any man be in Christ, he is a new creature; old things

are passed away; behold all things are become new. And all things are of God, who hath reconciled us to himself by Jesus Christ, and given to us the ministry of reconciliation. Hallelujah.

Actually, not only are we wonderfully made but because of Christ's death on the cross, we can also be wonderfully resorted to a right relationship with God. Basically, if anyone is in Christ, he is a new creation. Moreover, all this is from God almighty. Who reconciled us to Himself through Christ.

1 PETER 1 VS 13 Wherefore; gird up the loins of your mind, be sober; and hope to the end for the grace that is to be brought unto you at the revelation of Jesus Christ; Amen.

Basically, you are called to reign on this earth **[PSALM 24 VS 1]** Because the earth is of the Lord's and the fullness thereof; and the world that dwell therein. Actually, do you know who you are? Not an ordinary person. You are child of most high. Glory be to God almighty. Blackmail, lying about you, disappointment from people or some friends – these should have no place in you because you are God's temple on the earth. Almighty God wants to show His love through you. Literally, be bold to declare who you are and what you have. Moreover, if you can act like this, you will always find yourself walk in the realm of the miraculous.

REVELATION 5 VS 10 And hast made us unto our God King and Priest; and we shall reign on the earth.

Obviously, you have been called to reign in life as a King and Priest. Just CHILLOUT AND MAKE UP YOUR

MIND TO WALK, TALK AND LIVE AS THE King and Queen that you are. Refuse to talk cheap or live a beggarly life in opposition to what is to be expected from your so-called friends. Moreover, a King and Queen don't talk cheaply, they exercise authority. So my friends, BE YOURSELF.

> ISAIAH 58 VS 11 And the Lord shall guide thee continually, and satisfy thy soul in drought; and make fat thy bones; and thou shalt be like a watered garden, and like a spring of water; whose water fail Actually, you have an unfailing supply.

Whenever, you run out of answers and don't know what to do, He will reassure you.

> PSALM 32 VS 8 I will instruct thee and teach thee in the way which thou shall go; I will guide thee with mine eye.

> HEBREWS 12 VS 12 TO 15 Wherefore, lift up the hands which hang down, and the feeble knees; And make straight paths for your feet. Lest that which is lame be turned out of the way; but let it rather be healed. Follow peace with all man, and holiness, without which no man can see the Lord. Looking diligently lest any man fail of the grace of God; lest any root of bitterness spring up trouble you and thereby many be defiled.

When the load becomes too heavy to carry, you will hear His voice saying.

> PSALM 55 VS 22 Cast thy burden upon the Lord and he shall sustain thee, he shall never suffer the righteous to be moved.

Literally, who do you trust to solve your problem, God or yourself? Obviously, you need to live by the principle. However, do your best then let God handle the rest. As a matter of fact, so many people think that when they are facing challenges it's wrong to enjoy themselves. That is a lie from pit of hell.

> JOHN 16 VS 22 TO 24 And ye now therefore have sorrow; but I will see you again, and your heart shall rejoice, and your joy no man taketh from you. And in that day ye shall ask me nothing. Verily verily I say unto you [Ngozika] whatsoever ye shall ask the Father in my name; he will give to you. Hitherto have ye asked nothing in my name; ask ye shall receive that your joy may be full.

Obviously, if you remain faithful, God will lift you up in the midst of those who over looked and put you down, because you are now a new creation in Christ Jesus. However, a new creation means old things are passed away and all things are becoming new in your life. knowing that your life is in the hands of almighty God. Hallelujah. Literally, your mind is open to a new thing and your mind is renewed. Moreover, you think differently and you are focussed. However, you don't care what they say or what they think about you, because that's not the factor and it doesn't account. Our man of God said if you don't want people to talk about you, go at the back. Actually, can I be honest with you? You need Philistine and Pharaoh to reach your next level, that is where your potential will come out. Hallelujah.

> JEREMIAH 29 VS 11to14 And I know the thoughts that I think toward you, saith the Lord,

thoughts of peace, and not evil, to give you expected end. Then shall ye call unto me, and ye shall go and pray unto me and I will hearken unto you. And ye shall seek me, and find me, when ye shall search for me with all your heart. And I will be found of you, Saith the Lord; and I will turn away your captivity, and I will gather you from all the nations, and from all the places whither I have driven you, Saith the Lord; and I will bring you again into the place whence I caused you to be carried away captive.

Be Yourself, my beloved, we are free to be us because when you are yourself, it will enable you to love yourself. Actually, when you love yourself, you will develop a good attitude to love someone else because you cannot give what you don't have. Obviously, when you *be yourself*, you will develop confidence in yourself knowing that with God all things are possible to them that believe, because God cannot lie. Hallelujah. I am a living testimony. However, I love me, and I like to be me, which will save me from the hands of people and unfriendly friends.

However, you don't expect everybody to celebrate your success, as a matter fact you have to fight to get your destiny, and you have to fight to hold on to it. Actually, you can't coast on old victories, with each new battle. Basically, with each new battle you have to get fresh instruction. David inquired of the Lord saying, shall I go against the Philistines? However, the Lord said; go up for I will deliver the Philistines in to your hands. Literally, you have to remember the moment you lift up your head above the crowd you will attract attention. You have to learn from the duck, he stays calm on the surface, and keeps paddling underneath and lets the water run off him.

JOHN 1 VS 46] Nathanael said unto him, can any good thing come out of Nazareth? Philip saith unto him, come and see. Nathanael did and he ended up becoming a disciple. Moreover, often as events unfold, the cause of criticising will become clear and you will be vindicated. However, you must keep going because that is one of the packages in life, if you need to succeed.

Obviously, nobody had more critics than Paul. Yet he wrote; if God be for us, who can be against us.

Put this in your mind, ALL THINGS ARE WORKING TOGETHER FOR YOUR GOOD, NO MATTER WHAT, GOOD OR BAD, IS FOR YOUR GOOD. DON'T BE COMPLAINING OR MURMURING. JUST STAY FOCUSSED. AND TRUST GOD. God hates murmuring.

PSALM 71 VS 21 Thou shalt increase my greatness, and comfort me on every side.

## LET US PRAY

Your word says: "will keep him in perfect peace whose mind is stayed on thee, because he trusteth in thee." The Lord gives strength to his people; the Lord blesses his people with you; Your word says: "Peace I leave with you; my peace I gives you. Do not let your heart be troubled and do not be afraid". Your word says: "The peace of God, which transcends all understanding will guard your hearts and your mind in Christ Jesus."

Our Lord and our God we need the peace which transcends understanding to settle my nerves and calm my mind. Instead of thinking about our fears and worries, help us to focus on your goodness, your faithfulness, your healing power, your forgiving heart. My God and my Lord, take up residence within us and fill us with your peace. Lord, show us what's robbing us of it. We really want to know, Father, so we can be specific in what we need to confess, what we need to commit to and what we need to change. We open ourself to you now. Lord teaches us the secret of lasting peace. Moreover, Lord, we thank you for whatever it will take to help us receive the peace you have so generously offered to us. Your word says: "Let the peace of Christ rule in your hearts."

Obviously, today we want to be ruled by your peace instead of our fear and worries. Therefore, we give all our concerns to you, trusting You to work them out for our good and Your glory. Actually, our God shall wipe away all tears from our eyes; and there shall be no more death, neither shall be any more pain; for the former things are passed away. Lord bless us with what we work for and grant us what we hope for. Moreover, surprise us with what we have not asked for. In Jesus name we pray. Amen.

*"Never speak from the reality of your circumstances but speak from God's future perspective. Very important."*

**Vivian Rodgers**

PSALM 24 VS 1 You are called to reign on this earth because the earth is the Lord's and the fullness therefore; the world and they dwell therein.

Actually, do you know who you are? You are not an ordinary person; you are God's apple of his eyes. Moreover, be bold to declare who you are and what you have. Obviously, if you can act on this, you will always find yourself walking in the realm of miraculous. Actually, we are called to reign in life as a King and Priest. As a matter of fact, make up your mind to walk, talk and live as the King and Queen that you are. Basically, refuse to talk cheap or live a beggarly life because almighty God has made us King and priest in this world. Literally, A King and a Queen don't talk cheaply; they exercise authority given to them by almighty God.

> REVELATION 5 VS 10 And hast made us unto our God King and Priest; and we shall reign on the earth.

However, look what God promises us, when we live a life that pleases him.

> ISAIAH 43 VS 4 to 7 Since thou wast precious in my sight, thou hast been honourable and I have loved thee; therefore, will I give men for thee, and people for thy life. Fear not for I am with thee. I will bring thy seed from the east, and the north, and south; keep not back; bring my sons and my daughters from the end of the earth; even every one that is called by my name; for I have created him for my glory, I have formed him; yea, I have made him. So be yourself.

Basically, there were some Jewish men by name Shadrach, Meshach and Abednego.

> DANIEL 3 VS 16-30 They lived in Babylon in the city of King Nebuchadnezzar. It happened that this King build a golden image and he commanded that everybody will falleth down and worship this image. But these Jewish men refused to fall down and worship this golden

image. However, the King Nebuchadnezzar made a rule that whosoever fallen not down and worshipped shall the same hour be cast into the midst of a burning fiery furnace. Actually, the King was angry and he commanded them to bring Shadrach, Meshach, Abednego and asked: is it true that you did not serve my gods nor worship the golden image which I have set up? Then these Jewish men knew who they were and what they had inside. Moreover, they answered and said to the King: "We are not careful to answer thee in this matter. It be so, our God whom we serve is able to deliver us from the burning fiery furnace and he will deliver us out of thine hand O King. But if not, be it known unto thee O King that we will not serve thy gods nor worship the golden image which thou hast set up."

As a matter of fact, these Jewish men believed in themselves, and they knew who they were in Christ Jesus. Moreover, when you be yourself, you will not compromise, that is why they did not obey the King's order. However, they knew that the God they served was able to see them through. Hallelujah.

ACT 19 VS 20 So mightily grew the word of God and prevailed.

Actually, at the end of the matter King Nebuchadnezzar said, blessed be the God of Shadrach, Meshach, Abednego who hath sent his angel and delivered his servants that trusted in him and have changed the King's word and yielded their bodies that they might not serve nor worship any god except their own God. Moreover, the King made a decree; that every people nation and language which speak amiss against the God of Shadrach, Meshach and Abednego shall be made a dunghill because there is no other God can deliver after this sort. Then the King promoted Shadrach, Meshach and Abednego in the province of Babylon. Glory be to God almighty.

Basically, that is why you should be yourself. Nobody is able to take you out unless you permit them because you have the almighty God inside you. He said, The Lord is on your side so don't fear what man can do. Moreover, in the midst of your life changes and trials, remember that God is still at work in your life. Almighty God wants to use your tribulation to build your character and show you his glory.

> PSALM 118 VS 4 TO 6 Let them know that fear the Lord say, that his mercy endureth for ever called upon the Lord in distress; the Lord answer me and set me in a large place. The Lord is on my side will not fear what can man do to me?

> ROMANS 8 VS 34 to 39 Who is he that condemneth? It is Christ that died, yea rather; that is risen again, who is even at the right hand of God, who also maketh intercession for us. Who shall separate us from the Love of Christ? Shall tribulation, or distress, or perse-cution, or famine or nakedness peril, or sword? As it is written; For thy sake we are killed all the day long; we are accounted as sheep for the slaughter. Nay, in all these things we are more than conquerors through him that love us. For I am persuaded, that neither death, nor life, nor angels, nor principalities, nor powers nor

things to come, nor height, nor depth, nor other creature shall be able to separate us from the love of God, which is in Christ Jesus our Lord.

2 CORINTHIANS 2 VS 14 Now thanks be unto God, which always causeth us to triumph in Christ, and maketh manifest the saviour of his knowledge by us in every place.

1 SAMUEL, 17 VS 23 TO 54 Literally, there is one man by name David and his father's name is Jesse, and David was the youngest in their family. David took care of their sheep. David's three eldest brothers went to the battle front. One day the father asked David to go and visit his brothers and send them food. However, as he was talking with his brothers, the champion of the Philistines, Goliath by name came out of the armies of the Philistines, and spoke according to the same words; and David heard them. And the men of Israel, when they saw the man, they fled from him and were sore afraid.

Obviously, David was a man who could be himself and he was a man of faith. David spoke to those that stood by him, saying: Israel what shall be done to the man that killeth this Philistine and taketh away the reproach from? For who is this uncircumcised Philistine, that he should defy the armies of our living God?

Actually, whenever you take a stand and known you are in Christ people always criticise you. However, that is why you don't take notice of any body, that is why you have to be yourself, known if God be with you who then can be against you. Moreover, don't be a people pleaser. As a matter fact look at David's siblings, who criticised him. David's older brothers were angry and said to David: why comest thou down hither and with whom hast thou left those few sheep in the wilderness? Moreover, they even said to him: know thy pride and the naughtiness of thine heart, for thou art come down that thou mightiest see the battle.

Obviously, when you know who you are, people and your sibling opinion will not stop you. However, David did not mind his brother's attitude to stop him he even made up his mind to go and see Saul. Literally, look at the audacity of David, because he believed in himself and he had confidence in himself. As a matter of fact, look at what David said to Saul: let no man's heart fail because of him. Thy servant will go and fight with this Philistine. Saul didn't believe David, but David believed in himself. Saul said to David: thou are not able to go against this Philistine to fight with him, because thou are but a youth and this Philistine is a man of war from his youth.

Moreover, David knew who he was and the confidence he had in his God and he always *be himself*. Basically, imagine what David told Saul, He is giving his testimony, thy servant kept his father's sheep and there came a lion and bear and took a lamb out of the flock and I went out after him and smote him and derived it of his mouth. And when he arose against me, I caught him by his beard and smote him and slew him. As a matter of fact, thy servant slew both the lion and the bear. David is a man of faith and he knows what he has inside of him. He told Saul and said this uncircumcised Philistine shall be as one of them seeing he hath defied the armies of the living God. Hallelujah. David said again: moreover; the Lord that delivered me out of the paw of the lion and out of paw of the bear, he will deliver me out of this Philistine. Certainly, in life when you trust God and be yourself, God will show up for you because he knows you have confidence in him.

Obviously, when the Philistine saw David and he said am I a dog, that thou comest to me with staves? He was looking at David with the eyes of a little man, not knowing that David is a man after God's heart and a man of faith, who knows he can do all thing through Christ who strengthens him. (And his grace is sufficient for me and my power is made perfect in my weakness.) Actually, the Philistine made a statement to David: come to me and I will give thy flesh unto the fowls of the air and the beast of the field. However, David who knew what he has inside, said to the Philistine: thou come to me with a sword, but I come to thee in the name of our Lord of host, the God of the armies of Israel, who thou hast defied.

Basically, David believes in himself but Saul didn't believe in him because he felt he was not a man who could fight Goliath. David stood on the word of God – if God be for me, who then can be against me? Hallelujah. Literally, David prevailed over the Philistine with a sling and with a stone and smote the Philistine and slew him but there was no sword in the hands of David. However, David ran and stood upon the Philistine and took his sword and drew it out of the sheath thereof and slew him and cut off his head. As a matter of fact, when the Philistines saw their Champion was dead, they all fled.

Obviously, there are some key things to consider in this passage of scripture. First, the battle David was up against was impossible by natural standards. He was facing an enemy, Goliath, who was versed in the art of war, having been a soldier from the time he was young. He was bigger, and stronger and more experienced than David, who was an inexperienced teenager. As a matter of fact, from a natural, military perspective, David could easily have been humiliated by the larger and stronger Goliath. Moreover, Saul was telling David he wouldn't be successful in the battle because of his inexperience. Basically, how many times have you faced a situation that looked impossible? Moreover how many times have you been in the midst of a battle and the enemy told you the odds were against you? Actually, believe all of us have been there.

ISAIAH 54 VS 1 TO 7 Sing, O barren, thou that didst nor bear; break forth into singing, and cry aloud, thou that didst not travail with child; for more are the children of the desolate than the children of the married wife, saith the Lord. Enlarge the place of thy tent, and let them stretch forth the curtains of thine habitations spare not, lengthen thy cords, and strengthen. For thou shalt break forth on the right hand and on the left; and thy seed shall inherit the Gentiles, and make the desolate cities to be inhabited. Fear not; for thou shalt; not be ashamed; neither be thou confounded; for thou shalt not be put to shame for thou shalt forget the shame of thy youth, and shalt not remember the reproached of thy widowhood anymore. For thy Maker is thine husband the Lord of hosts is his name; and thy Redeemer the Holy One of Israel; The God of the whole earth shall be called. For the Lord hath called thee as a woman forsaken and grieved in spirit and a wife of youth, when thou wast refused saith thy God. For a small moment have I forsaken thee; but with great mercies will I gather thee.

Literally, David's response held the answer to why he won this battle. David responded to the challenge and the impending battle with faith and confidence in God. However, if David listened to his brothers, he could have missed his destiny. That is why you always *be yourself*, don't let anybody's criticisms stop you because not everybody will love you or accept you. Moreover, when God elevates you, it attracts so many haters, anyway you have to realize when your level changes, it is not everybody who is going with you. Therefore, accept their rejection, lies, blackmail and their frustration and move on because you are now on another level. Moreover, don't let anybody make you lose your cool, learn to enjoy yourself, love who you are nobody will love for you because *I love me* is all that matters, and *God loves me too*.

> PSALM 121 VS 1 TO 8 I will lift up mine eyes unto the hills, from hence cometh my help. My help cometh from the Lord, which made heaven and earth. He will not suffer thy foot to be moved, he that keepeth [Ngozi] shall neither slumber nor sleep. The Lord is thy keeper; the Lord is thy shade upon thy right hand. The sun shall not smite thee by day nor the moon by night. The Lord shall preserve thee from evil, he shall preserve thy soul. The Lord shall preserve thy going out and coming in from this time forth, and even for evermore. Amen.

Actually, when you allow the word entrance into your heart, fear and doubt melt away and faith takes over. The word of God in you will give you the mindset of the righteous and cause strength and boldness.

> PSALM 119 VS 133 to 135 Order my steps in thy

word; and let not any inequity have dominion over me. Deliver me from the oppression of man; so, will I keep thy precepts. Make Thy face to shine upon thy servant and teach me thy statutes.

PSALM 119 VS 130 The entrance of thy word giveth light; it giveth light; it giveth understanding unto the simple.

Be yourself is all about you knowing who you are and set others free.

REVELATION 3 VS 15 TO 16 I know thy works, that thou art neither cold nor hot; I would thou wert cold or hot. So then because thou art lukewarm; and neither cold nor hot, I will spue thee out of my mouth.

Moreover, almighty God hates a lukewarm person; that is why you have to *be yourself.*

Obviously, there was a story about Peter and John. **[ACT 3 VS 2 TO 7]** They were going to the gate of the temple which is called beautiful. On their way they met a certain man lame from his mother's womb. He was asking for alms. Peter, fastening his eyes upon him with John, said look on us, and he gave heed unto them, expecting to receive something of them. Then he said: "silver and gold have I none; but such as I have I give thee, and in the name of Jesus of Nazareth rise up and walk and he took him by the right hand lifted him up; and immediately his feet and ankle bones received strength. However, these are the men who knew what they have, Christ in them the hope of their glory. Actually, they didn't mind what people will say or what they think about them because they know who they are in Christ. Moreover, they are being self-knowing with God on their side they can move any mountain. Therefore, be yourself."

> JOHN 14 VS 11 TO 14 Believe me that I am in the Father, and the Father in me or else believe me for the very works' sake; Verily verily I say unto you, He that believe in me, the works that do shall he do also; and greater works than these shall he do, because I go to my Father; And whatsoever ye shall ask in my name, that will I do, that the Father may be glorified in the son. If ye shall ask any thing in my name, I will do it.

> 1 JOHN 5 VS 11 TO 12 And this is the record that God hath given to us eternal life, and this life is in his Son. He that hath the son hath life and he that hath not Son of God hath not life.

> 1 JOHN 5 VS 14 And this is the confidence that we have in him that, if we ask anything according to his will, he heareth us

As a matter of fact, with all these promises from God, you have known God cannot lie. Don't be a people pleaser, just be yourself, you are blessed of God. You are superior to Satan and his mother-in-law. You are no ordinary person. You are special, made by God almighty. Moreover, you have understood that someone's opinion of you does not be your reality. Actually, if there is no enemy within, the enemy outside can't do us any harm. Moreover, our friends will be nice to us, but our enemies will promote us. Basically, you have to know who you are in Christ, a child of most high. However, you have to know Christ lives inside you and Christ in you is the hope of your glory. Hallelujah. Literally, Paul described his deficiency as a thorn in the flesh that kept him humble. Paul asked God to remove it from him. God said: Paul be yourself; my grace is sufficient for you. For my strength is made perfect in your weakness. God's strength is best seen in our weakness. Moreover, our character of our words, is in your life. Actually, victors don't complain. Victors are never defeated. Obviously, always keep the word of God in your mouth, and keep the joy in your heart. As a matter of fact, do not be afraid or discouraged, because there is a greater power with us, than with them.

> LUKE 9 VS 1 Then he called his twelve disciples together and gave them power and authority over all devils and to cure diseases.

Moreover, the same is given to you, so act on it and take over. Basically, you don't give up hope, you have to fight for your life. You have to believe in yourself. Most likely you don't let others believe it for you. Use your word to rule your world. Almighty God doesn't react to your tears, God reacts to your faith.

> JOB 22 VS 28 Thou shall decree a thing, and it shall be established unto thee.

Are you aware it does not matter what challenges you face or how people think about you? However, they don't count and they are not the factor. You will remember there is power in your mouth, because once it goes out, it will accomplish what you said. Moreover, you will have what you said.

> ISAIAH 55 VS 11 So shall my word be that goeth forth out of my mouth; it shall not return unto me void, but it shall accomplish that which I

please; and it shall prosper in the things that whereto I sent it.

> MARK 11 VS 22 TO 24 And Jesus answering saith unto them. Have faith in God. For verily I say unto you. That whosoever shall say unto this mountain. Be thou removed. And be thou cast into the sea and shall not doubt in his heart, but shall believe that those things which he saith shall come to pass; he shall have whatsoever he saith.

Obviously, if you ever feel discouraged, downcast or rejected, all you have to do is consciously activate the Joy of the Lord from within and you will be strengthened. Moreover, you don't have to wait for anything or anybody to make you Joyful. Evoke Joy from within. Literally never you be dissatisfied or unhappy because of the challenging circumstances you might be facing or the ill treatment you get from others. It doesn't matter, you have to realise you are more than a conqueror. Actually, there is no adversity can overwhelm you. Obviously, when trouble comes, remember who you are, a child most high. That no weapon that formed against you shall prosper. Paul said: none of these things move me. Moreover, remind yourself of past victories, make a list of your blessings and read them out loud anytime you feel you are starting to sink emotionally.

> ACT 20 VS 24 But none of these things move me, neither count I my life dear unto myself that I might finish my course with Joy and the ministry which I have received of the Lord Jesus to testify the gospel of the God.

Actually, what made me write *Be Yourself* was because I faced a lot of persecution, blackmail, criticism from people I looked up to. But I never let it move me because I knew who I was in Christ Jesus. Challenges bring you down to your knees and make you want to pray every day, and problems make you come close to God. However never turn your back on God – that is when you need him more than any other time. With God all things are possible. Basically, never worry about anything because God is in control; and don't take any notice about how people will react to you or how you are feeling about your reputation, when people plan to bring you down; God knows who you are, that all matters. Moreover, look blackmail, rejection, persecution, and criticism as opportunities because it is there you will discover your purpose. Literally, never put too much value on what others have said; they are probably just projecting their frustration onto you. In fact, spend time with the right people. Whenever, you have optional time, spend it with those who build you up, not tear you down. Quality time with the right people will strengthen your faith and fortify you against the effects of the worst criticism. Moreover, it will also keep you from becoming critical of yourself.

Actually, look at David and his brothers, who criticised him when he was bringing food for them in the battlefield. When he saw Goliath, he wasn't thinking of becoming a hero, he just seized an opportunity an opportunity that other solders only dream about. The opportunity will catch you by surprise and if you are not alert and ready, you will miss it. Opportunity once lost can never be regained.

The story of Paul and Silas **[ACT 15 VS 25 TO 28]** helps you to stand more in God.

ACT 20 VS 24 But none of these things move me, neither count I my life dear unto myself, so that I might finish my course with Joy and the ministry which I have received of the Lord Jesus to testify the gospel of the grace of God.

EPHESIANS 3 VS 20 Now unto him that is able to do exceedingly abundantly above all that we ask or thing, according to the power that is worketh in us.

Paul and Silas went out to pray and on the way they met one woman that was possessed with a spirit of divination. Moreover, she had the gift of soothsaying and she used the gift to make money for her master; however when she noticed Paul and Silas, she cried out saying: these men are the servants of the most high, you know you cannot cover the light. Paul being grieved, he turned and said to the spirit: I command thee in the name of Jesus Christ, come out of her. And the same hour the spirit left her.

Obviously, the master was angry because he would not make money again. Literally, the master went after Paul and Silas and caught them and brought them to a magistrate and said these men being Jews do exceedingly trouble our city. Moreover, they teach customs, which are not lawful for us to receive, neither to observe, being Roman. As a matter of fact, a multitude rose up together against them; and the magistrates rent up their clothes and commanded to beat them. Actually, when they had laid many stripes on them, they cast them into prison he charging the jailer to keep them safely. However, at midnight Paul and Silas prayed and sang praises unto God and the prisoners heard them, and suddenly there was a great earthquake, that the foundations of the prison were shaken and immediately all the doors opened. Then, the jailer, waking up from sleep and seeing the prison doors open, drew out his sword and would have killed himself, supposing that the prisoners had fled. Basically, Paul cried with a loud voice saying: do yourself no harm for we are all here. Moreover, these men of God didn't feel sorry for themselves. Most likely they did not ask "God why me?" Moreover, they were beaten and had their clothes rent and were put in prison in the midst of their challenges, they sang and praised God.

> PSALM 125 VS 1 They that trust in the Lord shall be as mount Zion, which cannot be removed; but abided for ever.

> PSALM 23 VS 4 Yea through the valley of the shadow of death. I fear no evil; for thou art with me thy rod and thy staff they comfort me.

> PSALM 25 VS 1 to 3 Unto thee; O Lord do I lift up my soul my God I trust in thee; let me not be ashamed. Let not mine enemies triumph over me. Yea, let none that wait on thee be ashamed, let them be ashamed which transgress without cause.

> PSALM 27 VS 5 TO 6] For in the time of trouble he shall hide me in his pavilion; in the secret of his tabernacle shall he hide me; he shall set me up upon a rock. And now shall mine head be lifted up above mine enemies round about me; there will offer in his tabernacle sacrifices of Joy; I will sing praises unto the Lord.

> MARK 9 VS 23 Jesus said unto him if thou

canst believe; all things are possible to him that believeth.

MATTHEW 17 VS 20 And Jesus said unto them: Because of your unbelief; for verily I say unto you, if ye have faith as a grain of a mustard seed, ye shall you say unto this mountain. Remove hence to yonder place; and it shall remove; and nothing shall be impossible unto you.

Literally, there was one family in the Bible by name Elimelech and Naomi. They had two sons by name Mahion and Chilion. And they had wives by name Ruth and Orpah. However, there was a famine in the town of Bethlehem and they decided to leave and stay in the land of Moab. Basically, unexpected tragedy happened to this family in the land of Moab. Naomi's husband died and her two sons died. Unfortunately, Naomi could not handle the situation. She was so sad that she changed her name to Mara "because almighty God hath dealt very bitterly with me". Most likely she decided to go back to the land of Judah. Moreover, Naomi was so sad that she asked her two daughters-in-law to return each to her mother's house, but Ruth said: entreat me not to leave thee or to return from following after thee, therefore for whither thou goes I will go and where thou goes I will go. Actually, in life rain falls on the unjust and just. Yes, that is why you have to be yourself, knowing that in everything give thanks to God because God is God of second chances. Obviously, check out how God turned it around for Ruth when she got in contact with Boaz. Ruth found favour in the eyes of Boaz. However, God remembered the house of Naomi by giving her a son. They named him Obed; Glory be to God almighty. God saw from beginning to the end. Literally, you see how God operated; even in disappointment, there is an opportunity, which is why you don't give up in life. As a matter of fact, could it be that if Ruth had gone back to her father's house there would be nothing like the father of Jesse and father of David? History couldn't be born. Certainly, in every tragedy there is hope.

However, in life you cannot change the past but you can do something about the future. Obviously, what's in front of you is more significant than what's behind you.

> ISAIAH 55 VS 8 TO 9 For my thoughts are not your thoughts, neither are your ways my ways saith the Lord. For as heavens are higher than the earth, so are my ways higher than your ways, and my thoughts than your thoughts.

> PSALM 126 VS 1 TO 6 When the Lord turned against the captivity of Zion, we were like them that dream. Then was our mouth filled with laughter, and our tongue with singing; then said they among the heathen, the Lord hath done great things for them.

Authentically, the Lord hath done great things for us; whereof we are glad. Turn again our captivity Lord as the streams in the south. They that sow in tears shall reap in Joy. He that goeth forth and weepeth. bearing precious seed, shall doubtless come again with rejoicing, bringing his sheaves with him.

> 1 CORINTHIANS 9 VS 24 The Bible says, know ye not that they which run in a race in all, but one receiveth the prize? So run that ye may obtain.

Literally, in life you only get to run once, so run to win. Moreover, to avoid stumbling or losing your place, don't look back. Actually, you can't change the past, but thank God you can learn from it and leave it behind. However, don't be anxious about the next lap, focus only on the next step. Very important, if you miss that step, you may fall and not get up again. Basically, before you know it, you will soon have more laps behind you than ahead of you so make every lap count. However, let us lay aside every weight and the sin which so easily ensnares us and let's run with endurance the race that is set before us. Actually, many of us carry the weight and worry of burdens that older and wiser people understand are of no real importance. As a matter fact, we spend our strength extinguishing fires that, if left alone would burn out on their own. Do you know that time is your most valuable resource? Save it and you have increased your assets and decreased your liabilities. Moreover, get rid of baggage of old relationships, pointless fears and false indebtedness to those who seek to manipulate you. Authentically, there are enough painful trials in life; why endure the ones you can lay aside? When blind Bartimaeus heard that Jesus was within reach he threw off his coat lest it trip him down, and ran, therefore, toward Him. And his faith paid off; immediately he received his sight and followed Jesus Christ. Hallelujah. Therefore, today lay it aside and run.

Actually, to be successful in anything God calls you to do, you must be sensitive to the Holy Spirit within you and learn to recognise when He speaks to you through the scriptures.

Obviously, when pressure is on and you are tempted to move too quickly you will hear His voice saying, **[ISAIAH 52 VS 12]** For ye shall not go out with haste nor go by flight; for the Lord will go before you; and the God of Israel will be your reward.

Literally, do you know that God has got you covered, front and back. How good is that? Most likely when you are about to make a wrong turn or a bad decision, He will remind you a man's heart deviseth his ways but the Lord directs to get the job done, His voice will whisper. God cannot lie, his words are yea and amen.

> PSALM 37 VS 4 to 5 Delight thyself also in the Lord; and he shall give thee the desires of thine heart. Commit the why unto the Lord; trust also in him; and he shall bring it to pass.

> ISAIAH 58 VS 11 And the Lord shall guide thee continually, and satisfy thy soul in drought, and make fat thy bones and thou shalt be like a watered garden and like spring of water whose waters fail not. You have an unfailing supply.

> Basically, you run out of answers and don't know what to do, He will reassure you.

> PSALM 32 VS 8 I will instruct thee and teach thee in the way which thou shall go; I will guide thee with mine eye.

Actually, when the load becomes too heavy to carry, you will hear His saying.

> PSALM 55 VS 22 Cast thy burden upon the Lord and he shall sustain thee, he shall never suffer the righteous to be moved.

Hearing God's voice may mean you have to sacrifice lesser things and tune out other voices. But you must do it – it is more important than learning to recognise God's voice when He speaks to you. There is one place in the

Bible I like to read when I want to keep my mind at rest.

> ISAIAH 26 VS 3 to 4 Thou will keep him in perfect peace, whose mind is stayed on thee; because he trusted in thee. Trust ye in the Lord Jehovah, his everlasting strength.

Obviously, who are you trusting to solve your problem, God or yourself? Moreover, you need to live by the principle. Do your best, then let God do the rest. Too many of us think that it's wrong to enjoy ourselves while we have problems.

> PSALM 80 VS 19 Turn us again, God of hosts; cause thy face to shine; and we shall be saved.

> JOHN 16 VS 22 to 24 And ye now therefore have sorrow; but I will see you again, and your heart shall rejoice, and your joy no man taketh from you. And in that day ye shall ask me nothing. Verily verily I say unto [Ngozika] whatsoever ye shall ask the father in my name, he will give it to you, hitherto have ye asked nothing in my name; ask, and ye shall receive that your joy may be full.

> ISAIAH 26 VS 9 With my soul have I desired thee in the night; yea, with my spirit within me I seed thee early; for when thy judgments are in the earth, the inhabitants of the world will learn righteousness.

Obviously, keeping your peace doesn't exempt you from life's difficulties, it just allows God to have the last word. By trusting Him completely, you are no longer at the mercy of circumstances, other people, or your own emotions and limitations. Actually, because of what happened to me in London, it resulted in me writing a book *Coming to London*. Their plan is for me to lose confidence and to kill my dreams in ministry, but the devil is a liar, greater is He that is in me, than any of them that is in the world. Moreover, in life never devalue yourself. You have to know your worth; literally, just because someone else didn't see your value, doesn't mean you are worthless; as a matter fact, you will never succeed with people who devalue you. Child of most high, you are valuable, you are God special, never allow anybody to make you feel inadequate. Learn to be yourself.

> 1 PETER 2 VS 9 But ye are a chosen generation, a royal priesthood, an holy nation, a peculiar people; that ye should shew forth the praises of him who hath called you out of darkness into his marvellous light.

> HEBREWS 10 VS 35 TO 39 Cast not away therefore your confidence, which hath great recompense of reward. For ye have need of patience that after ye have done the will of God, ye might receive the promise. For yet a little while, and he that shall come will come and tarry. Now the just live by faith; but if any man draw back, my soul shall have no pleasure in him. But we are not of them who draw back unto perdition; but of them that believe to the saving of the soul.

> ROMANS 8 VS 31 TO 37 What shall we them say to these things? If God be for us, you then can be against you, know that nothing can separate you

from the love of God.

> ROMANS 8 VS 35 Who shall separate us from the love of Christ? Tribulation, blackmail, distress persecution or famine or nakedness, or peril or sword. ? As it is written, for thy sake we are killed all the day long; we are accounted as sheep for slaughter. Nay, in all these we are more than conquerors through him that love us.

Literally, you don't talk of yourself according to the way you feel or look. Be optimistic and speak the word of God over your life. Moreover, don't say to yourself what others says, unless it worth repeating. Maybe people decide to undo you with lies and blackmail. Obviously, they may not know any better because everybody has the right of their own opinion. Authentically, the good news is you don't have to be affected by their words for the rest of your life. Actually, you need not change the image of yourself to please people. However, you are not calling for everybody and not everybody will except you. Learn to be yourself because rain falls to just and unjust. Know whose you are, because you are the light of the world. Basically, you are too loaded to be molested. Obviously, never be intimidated by their words because this shall pass. Moreover, don't give them attention, always put your trust in God almighty and his word. Actually, the word of God is in the womb of your miracle. So, speak the word of God; it's never failed, it is life to a dying body,

> PSALM 18 VS 30 TO 40 As for God; his way is perfect; the word of the Lord is tried; he is a buckler to all those that trust in him. For who is God save the Lord? Or who is a rock save our God? It is God that girdeth me with strength,

and maketh my way perfect. He maketh my feet like hind's feet and setteth me upon my high places. He teacheth my hands to war, so that a bow of steel is broken by mine arms. Thou hast also given me the shield of thy salvation; and thy right hand holdeth me up and thy gentleness hath made me great. Thou slip. I have pursued mine enemies; and overtaken them; neither did I turn again till they were consumed. I have wounded them they were not able to rise; they strength unto the battle; thou hast girded me with strength unto the battle; thou hast also given me the necks of mine enemies; that I might destroy them that hate me.

Actually, you have to get into agreement with Him. David said my confidence is in the Lord and you can say the same thing. Paul said: we can do all things through Christ who strengthens us. Literally, you have to speak the word because God does not give us the spirit of fear.

2 TIMOTHY 1 VS 6 TO 7 Wherefore I put thee in remembrance that thou stir up the gift of God, which is in thee by putting on my hands. For God hath not given us the spirit of fear; but of power and of love and of a sound mind.

2 CORINTHIANS 3 VS 4 TO 6 And such trust have we through Christ to God-ward; Not that we are sufficient of ourselves to think anything as of ourselves; but our sufficiency is of God; Who also hath made us able ministers of the New Testament; not of letter; but of the spirit for the letter killeth, but the spirit giveth life.

2 CORINTHIANS 1 VS 20 For all the promises of God in him are yea, and in him Amen, unto the glory of God by us. Now he which establisheth us with you in Christ; and hath anointed us, is God.

2 CORINTHIANS 3 VS 16 TO 17 Nevertheless when it shall turn to the Lord, the vail shall be taken away, Now the Lord is that Spirit and, where the Spirit of the Lord is there is liberty. But we all with open face beholding as in a glass the glory of the Lord are changed into the same image from glory to glory, even as by the Spirit of Lord.

MATTHEW 5 VS 45 That ye may be the children of your Father which is in heaven; for he maketh his sun to rise on the evil and on the good, and sendeth rain on the just and unjust.

MATTHEW 5 VS 14 Ye are the light of the world. A city that is set on a hill cannot be hid.

Moreover, if you feel discouraged from any source that isn't God sending it your way, immediately reject it and if you have no other source of encouragement, then just do what David did by encouraging himself in the Lord. Actually, when you notice that you are losing courage, talk to yourself, tell yourself you have made it through difficulties in the past and victories will be had again. If you don't give up. Moreover, make a list of your blessings and read them out loud anytime you feel you are emotionally down, it will help you, Bible said count your blessings; name them one by one and you will see what God has done for you.

Obviously, if we are not busy trying to avoid personal pain, fear, and anger, we could help others. Perhaps we should once and for all put ourselves in God's capable hands, telling Him how we feel and what happened to us. Moreover, that will help us to develop confidence in ourselves. Honestly, many times our outward appearance shows the way we are feeling inside, But it can also work the other way; When we look confident on the outside, we can feel more confident on the inside. Actually, don't slump your shoulders and hang your head down. Do you know you are full of God life? So act like it – live with passion, zeal and enthusiasm. However, don't just try to make it through the day, celebrate the day and say this is the day the Lord has made – we will rejoice and be glad in it. As a matter of fact, don't dread the day, attack the day, know what you want to accomplish today and go for it.

PSALM 118 VS 24 This is the day which the Lord hath made: we will rejoice and be happy in it Authentically, don't live constantly comparing yourself with others. Be yourself and celebrate who God has made you to be. Moreover, there is only one who has the unique traits and skills that make up who you are. Actually, be yourself, God knew what He was doing and so rely on the thought that surely God said something about you as He did when He called the world in to creation. And it was good. Obviously, you must express your faith when you pray. Moreover, you must believe the word of God in your spirit. Faith makes you a possessor. As a matter of fact, having faith in God will make you to have no regrets of yesterday because the regrets of yesterday and fear of tomorrow are enemies of today's happiness. Literally, God doesn't live in your yesterday and He doesn't triumph in your fears. However, He expects you to be yourself and enjoy the simple little things of life that God has given to you. Moreover, for you to enjoy your spiritual realities, you first start out by appreciating yourself and then also people God has placed in your world. Most likely you can learn to let go of your past experiences, especially the unpleasant ones and have no fret or tear of tomorrow.

PSALM 138 VS 8 The Lord will perfect that which concerneth me; thy mercy O Lord, endureth for ever, forsake not works of thine own hands.

PSALM 37 VS 24 TO 25 Though he fall, he shall not utterly cast down; for the Lord upholdeth him with his hand. Have been young and now am old; yet have I not seen the righteous forsake; nor his seed begging bread.

Basically, I realised we should not live in fear and not worry about our future because He is going to perfect that which concerns us. Obviously, that is why you have to rejoice because the Holy Spirit will perfect everything about your life. Therefore, chill out, and be yourself. Our almighty God said: I came that they may enjoy life and have it more abundant life till it overflows.

JOHN 10 VS 10 The thief cometh not, but for to steal and to kill, and to destroy; I am come that they might have life and that they might have it more abundantly,

1 PETER 5 VS 7 Casting thy burden upon him for he careth for you.

PSALM 55 VS 22 Casting thy burden upon the Lord and he shall sustain thee; he shall never suffer the righteous to be moved. Amen.

Therefore, leave everything in the hands of the Lord. He's powerful enough to handle them. When the almighty God said that those things that concern us. He is going to perfect it, that is why you have to trust Him with all your heart and soul, and give your life to God. Moreover, make Him your first priority. And when this happens in your life you will experience His peace which passes understanding. As a matter of fact, when you know the word of God for yourself, it will help you to meditate on it day and night.

JOSHUA 1 VS 8 to 9 This book of the law shall not depart out thy mouth but thou shall meditate therein day and night, that thou mayest observe to do according to all that is written therein ; for thou shalt make thy way prosperous, and then thou shall have good success. Have not I commanded thee? Be strong and of good courage; be not afraid neither be dismayed; for the Lord thy God is with thee whither so ever thou goest. Amen.

Obviously, that is why you have to look for a good church where they will teach you the word of God in your spirit, not miracles. Moreover, you need to understand the Bible first. Miracle is good, because our father Jesus believes in miracles; He does a lot of miracles. Why do you need to know the word of God for yourself? Because the evil days are coming, and who will you cal? Actually, God said: I have given you power to cast out devils and whatsoever you ask in my name I will do it for you, so that the father will be glorified. Not only was your pastor given the power, it was given to you too so you know what do in case of challenges coming. However, when you know the word of God in your spirit, it will enable you not to run from one church to another. Also there are so many Christian books out there you can read. It's helpful. I have read a lot of books and I learnt a lot through those books.

> 2 TIMOTHY 2 VS 15 Study to shew thyself approved unto God, a workman that needeth not to be ashamed, rightly dividing the word of truth.

Literally, even Daniel believed in reading books.

> DANIEL 9 VS 2 In the first year of his reign, I Daniel understand by books the number of the year, whereof the word of the Lord came to Jeremiah the prophet, that he would accomplish seventy years in the desolations of Jerusalem.

Actually, a read is a lead.

> DANIEL 5 VS 14 I have even heard of thee, that the spirit of God is in thee, and that light and understanding and excellent spirit wisdom is found in thee.

> DANIEL 6 VS 3 Then this was preferred above the presidents and princes because an excellent spirit was in him, and the King thought to set him over the whole realm.

> HOSEA 4 VS 6 My people are destroyed for

lack of knowledge, because thou hast rejected knowledge will also reject thee, that thou be no priest to me. Seeing thou hast forgotten the law of God, I will also forget thy children.

Basically, in life you never know what you will come across, but if you know the word of God in your spirit, there is no challenge you cannot handle. Actually, that is why God told Joshua this book of law should not depart out of your mouth. Moreover, the same principle applies to us today if we believe, to meditate on the word, not our trouble. For example, because of what I have been through in London, it made me write this book. As a matter of fact, if I hadn't known the word of God my spirit could have lost my mind. But thanks be to God for his Mercy and Grace, that I am still standing by his grace. God is God of justice.

PSALM 66 VS 12 Thou hast caused men to ride over my heads; we went through water but thou broughtest us out into a wealthy place.

PSALM 46 VS 1 God is our refuge and strength, a very present help in trouble.

PSALM 46 VS 5 God is in midst of her; she shall not be moved; God shall help her, and that right early.

PSALM 46 VS 7 The Lord of hosts is with us; the God of Jacob is our refuge. Selah.

PSALM 46 VS 10 Be still and know that I am

God; I will be exalted in the earth. The Lord of hosts is with us; the God of Jacob is our refuge. Selah.

PSALM 97 VS 10 Ye that love the Lord, hate evil; he preserveth the souls of his saints; he delivered them out the hand of the wicked.

Moreover, never have you lived in fear about the unknowing enemies. The Holy Spirit is with you there. That is why God wants to perfect in all we do by us renewing our minds, by not speaking negative words.

PROVERB 18 VS 21 Death and life are in the power of the tongue; and they that love it shall eat the fruit thereof.

As a matter of fact, most people often use these words: *I am afraid of going out in the night*, or *I don't know what to do about my children*. Or *I don't know if God will answer my prayer*. Obviously, our talk should be confident and bold, not fearful talk. Fearful talk not only affects us in an adverse way, but affects those around us, Actually, if you will just change the way you talk, you will immediately begin to feel stronger, bolder, more courageous and less afraid. There was one prophet by name Elijah who called fire from heaven. But he ran away because of Jezebel. Out of fear.

1 KINGS 19 VS 1 to 3 And Ahab told Jezebel all that Elijah had done, and withal how he had slain all the prophets with the sword. Then Jezebel sent a messenger unto Elijah saying. So let the gods do to me, and more also, if I make not thy life as the life of one them by tomorrow about this time. And when he saw that, he arose,

and went for his life and came to Beer-Sheba; which belongeth to Judah and left his servant there. But he himself went a day's journey into the wilderness and he sat down under a juniper tree and he requested for himself that he might die; and said, It is enough; now. O Lord take away my life; for I am not better than my father.

Basically, do you see what fear can do, if you let it? A man who killed 450 false prophets, now lives in fear. He was afraid to go back to his house. He went and stayed in the wilderness. Fear made Elijah lose his confidence in God. He even wanted to commit suicide and lost his perspective. However, we should not live in fear. Fear is a spirit, whenever you notice fear, cast him out. Fear is an enemy. Most likely, whenever fear knocks on your door, open it with faith. Fear means to run away or to take flight, but confrontation means to face something head on. Sometimes confrontation requires us to face ourselves. Maybe we are fearful of failure or fearful of success. Obviously, I hate fear, and what it does to people. It makes us withdraw; it makes us retreat; it eats away our confidence and our self-assurance. Prayer does give us the strength to stand against fear, and to overcome and be conquerors like God intends us to be. However, we must have something to overcome and conquer. Literally, you would never expect to run three miles without first learning to run one. Obviously, it's the same way with prayers. At a matter of fact, God wants us to stretch our faith muscles and stand against fear. He wants us to say: no, fear is not going to rule in my life. Moreover, as we learn to use prayer to confront and combat the small fear, he will help us learn to tackle the bigger fear too. Don't let fear freeze you into paralysis.

JOHN 17 VS 15 I pray not that thou shouldest keep them from evil. They are not of the world, even as I am not of the world.

Authentically, it is possible to live in this world that is full of trouble, and chaos and yet not be troubled by it. In other words, what controls them, shouldn't control you, what destroys them, shouldn't destroy you. What limits them, shouldn't limit you. Why? Because as a follower of Christ, Jesus prayed that you would be protected from the evil one. There is something that separates you from the rest of the world. You are in it, but you are not of it. We can see this was true in the life of Job. For sure that is why the Bible said that God built a hedge around Job.

JOB 1 VS 10 Hast not thou made a hedge about him, and about his house and about all that he hath on every side? Thou hath blessed the work of his hands and his substance is increased in the land. Obviously, that means God insulated Job from the things that Satan wanted to do to him. In fact, Satan accuses God of protecting Job. The message translation records Satan as saying no one has ever had it so good. You make sure nothing bad ever happens to him or his possession. You bless everything he does; he can't lose. Satan was fully aware that Job had a hedge or wall of protection around him and couldn't penetrate in his house or his life. He even tried to get God to take it down but He wouldn't do it. This is very important. God wouldn't remove it, and Satan couldn't remove it. This means that the only one who could remove this wall of protection was Job himself. Moreover, you discover that Job eventually did remove this wall of protection by opening the spirit of fear. Actually, after the hedge came down and Job began to experience destruction on every side. He said:

JOB 3 VS 25 For the thing which I greatly feared is come upon me. I was not in safety, neither had I rest neither was I quiet; yet trouble came. This fear didn't start overnight, it having been inside Job's mind for a long time because of his bad children.

Fear is the opposite of faith.

2 CORINTHIANS 5 VS 7]For we walk by faith not by sight; We are confident say, and willing rather to be absent from the body, and to be present with the Lord.

HEBREW 11 VS 38 Now the just shall live by faith but if any man draw back, my soul shall have no pleasure in him.

HEBREW 19 VS 1 Now faith is the substance of things hoped for, the evidence of things not seen.

HEBREW 11 VS 6 But without faith it is impossible to please him; for he that cometh to God must believe that he is and that he is rewarded of them that diligently seek him.

HEBREW 11 VS 29 By faith they passed through the red sea as by dry land; which the Egyptians assaying to do were drowned.

HEBREW 11 VS 30 By faith the wall of Jericho

fell down, after they were compassed about seven days.

Actually, use your faith to create what you want. You can use our faith to rule our world. Moreover, with your faith in the word of God we will escape trouble. With your faith in the word, you will have good success, Through faith you can create what you want before you receive it. In fact, faith comes when you develop confidence in God, knowing that all things are working together for your good, and God cannot lie. Caleb was a man of faith, and had confidence in his self. He believed all things were possible with God. Basically, there was war in Amalekites, the people were giants who lived there. Moses sent some people to go and spy in the land of Canaan. Literally, people were afraid to go, but Caleb was a man of faith and he had confidence in himself.

> NUMBERS 13 VS 30 And Caleb stilled the people before Moses, and said, let us go up at once, and possess it; for we are well able to overcome it. But the men that went up with him said, we be not able to go up against the people; for they are stronger than we.

> NUMBERS 14 VS 6 TO 9 And Joshua the son of Nun and Caleb the son of Jephunneh, which were of them that searched the land, rent their clothes; And they spoke unto all the company of the children of Israel, saying, The land which we passed through to search it, is an exceeding good land. If the Lord delight in us; then he will bring us into this land, and give it us, a land which floweth with milk and honey. Only rebel not ye against the Lord, neither fear ye the people of the

land; for they are bread for us; their defence is departed from them and the Lord is with us; fear them not.

Obviously, these are men who have confidence in God, they know that if God is with them, nobody can be against them.

MARK 9 VS 23 Jesus said unto him, if thou canst believe, all things are possible to him that believeth.

1 CORINTHIANS 2 VS 9 But as it written, whatever the eye hath not seen, nor ear heard, neither have entered into the heart of man the things which God hath prepared for them that love him.

HEBREW 6 VS 19 That by two immutable things in which it was impossible for God to lie. We might have a strong consolation, who have filed for refuge to lay hold upon the hope set before us. Which hope we have as anchor of the soul, both sure and steadfast, and which entereth into that within the vail.

PHILIPPIANS 4 VS 6 to 7 Be careful for nothing but in everything by prayer and supplication with thanksgiving, let your requests be made known unto God.

Authentically, the word of God tells us be anxious; for nothing instead, in everything by prayer and supplication with thanksgiving you should make your request to God. And the peace of God which passeth all understanding shall keep your hearts and minds through

Christ Jesus. Moreover, learn to put your trust in God alone. and rest your faith on the word, for his word never fail. Obviously, focus to trust Him with confidence and assurance knowing that God is a faithful God. who never fail. Actually, the solution to every problem you face is contained in scripture. Obviously, to be wise you must study your book. To be successful in life, must practice it. Once you understand that your straggle will begin to make sense. Actually, as you study God's word, you will begin to experience the mind-renewing and life-changing power he has deposited with you; know him who is able to do immeasurably more than all we ask or imagine according to his power that is at work with us. So start drawing in the power today.

> PHILIPPIANS 4 VS 13 I can do all things through Christ which strengtheneth me.

Obviously, you must continually acknowledge that your strength isn't your physical abilities but, in the Lord, for without Him you can do nothing. Moreover, learn the value of meditation on the word of God. Basically, the word has the ability to create and produce opportunities and guidance for you. Honestly, the word of God in you enlarges your vision. Most likely refuse to see lack and want, look beyond the horizon and let the word propel you to prosperity. Authentically, if you build your faith strong in God's word, you will neither cry nor be cast down. Moreover, your faith grows when you do what He says. Always ask for God's wisdom, and never share your testimony to people you don't know, because the devil goes to church.

# ENCOURAGEMENT

Actually, people who are afraid of persecution, rejection, blackmail and reputation never finish well or win their battle. Moreover, they are worrying about what people say and because of that, they compromise and miss their destiny. To be honest, who cares what people say or think about you; all that matters is are you in the right place with your God because people who sing hosanna with you today may become the worst enemy you have in your life. Just think about Jesus and Judas Iscariot. Literally, never give up, never accept that you are a failure. Moreover, you are not a failure until you accept that you are one. Challenges are stepping stones to your miracle. Obviously, don't allow any obstacle to stop or discourage you, because out of every obstacle, there is a potential miracle. As a matter of fact, the challenge before you is to take you to a greater height. Do you know what Goliath did for David. **[1 SAMUEL 17]**

However, don't run away from any challenge that confronts you. Stand strong and tell yourself, "I can still make it". [WOW] As a matter of fact, let God be your first priority; moreover, never give up your dreams no matter what. Never be a quitter. Quitters never accomplish their assignment. Quitters never achieve their goals. Always inspire yourself. Obviously, never stay where they tolerate you, go where they celebrate you because you are the mirror of God, you are the righteousness of God. Actually, all it took was one daring decision; that's all it ever takes. O yes, God will move on your behalf. However, if you don't move, you will always wonder *what if?* Basically, our longest regrets are our inactions – regrets about the things we would have, could have or should have done but did not do.

Therefore, the word for you today is trust God and his words. Authentically, the choice you make today will determine your positions tomorrow and the seeds you sow today determine your harvest tomorrow. Most likely, you don't need anybody's approval because you are God chosen and God special. Glory be to God almighty. Obviously, learn to enjoy yourself because life is too short. Moreover, don't be a people pleaser. That will help you. However, remember that what you make happen to others, God will make happen to you, be it good or bad. Therefore, be good to people because the people you meet down, one day you will meet them up. God is not a respecter of persons. Literally, never put your trust in man, because man will disappoint you one day. However, you are the architect of yourself. Moreover, don't let your fear become your reality. Obviously, never worry about things you cannot change. Actually, don't allow people's opinion to affect you because you are wonderful made and God's workmanship. Created in his image. Halle-lujah. Authentically, never allow people's opinion to devalue you because nobody is better than you. It's only God's opinion that matters. People are people, God is God himself. Obviously, people like you the way you are, but when you come up high then it can become a problem. Do you know that not everybody will celebrate your new you. So be yourself. Remember this; new level new devil. Ha ha ha. To God be the glory. When they set to bring me down, I never knew such things would happen to me – not one, not two, not three. But I know there is God, the father to fatherless. The husband to the widow. The rock of my salvation. In proverb 24 VS 10 it is said: If you faint in the day of adversity, thy strength is too small. Apostle Paul said it is well for me: that I have been afflicted; that I mighty learn thy statutes **[PSALM 119 VS 71]** Affliction will help you discover your real you. Moreover, it enables you to discover the gift of God that is hiding in you. Hallelujah. Actually, that is why God said in everything give thanks, good or bad, I will be bold to take you. I am a living testimony. Glory be to God almighty.

> EXODUS 3 VS 7 to 9 And the Lord said, I have surely seen the affliction of my people which are in Egypt, and have heard their cry by reason of their taskmaster; for I know their sorrows; And I am come down to deliver them out of the hand of the Egyptians, and to bring them up out of that land unto a good land flowing with milk and honey; unto the place of the Canaanites, and the Hittites, and the Hivites, and the Jebusites.

> PROVERB 24 VS 5 A wise man is strong; yea a man of knowledge increaseth strength.

> MATTHEW 5 VS 14 Ye are the light of the world. A city that is set on a hill cannot be hid.

> MATTHEW 11 VS 12 And from the day of John Baptist until now Kingdom of heaven suffereth violent and the violent take it by force.

Obviously, those who can take it by force, are those who are ready to fight on their knees and not minding about what people say, because Christianity is a battle-field.

> EPHESIANS 6 VS 12 For we wrestle not against flesh and blood, but against principalities, against power, against the rulers of darkness of

this world, against wackiness in high places.

Literally, that is why you have to fight for your life. Moreover, you don't let your enemies have the last word on your life. In life, never you be a quitter. Quitters never accomplish their assignment. Quitters never win. Quitters never achieve their goal.

> PROVERB 16 VS 7 When a man's ways please the Lord, he maketh even his enemies to be at peace with him.

As a matter of fact, always inspire yourself. Never stay where they tolerate you, go where they celebrate you because you are the mirror of God and have God's righteousness in you. You don't need anybody to approve of you. God has approved of you. That's all matters.

Basically, you have to be yourself, love yourself, moreover if you are waiting for people to love, you will wait for a long time. If you cannot love yourself, hug yourself, nobody will love you for you. And if you are waiting for people to make you happy, you will wait for a long time because happiness comes from inside. However, you don't need so many people in your life, all you need is somebody who understands your passion and your goals. Never use the same weapon that your enemies use to fight you. Never go with the crowd, the crowd either makes you or destroys you. Eagles never go with crowd, but always fly alone. But turkeys go with the crowd, because they don't know where they belong, that is why they can tolerate any nonsense. When you know who you are in God, nobody can take your place in God or bring you down. Moreover, when God bless nobody curse. When God lift up, nobody can bring down. God cannot lie.

COLOSSIANS 2 VS 10 And ye are complete in

him, which is the head of all principality and power.

COLOSSIANS 3 VS 2 TO 3 Set your affection on things above, not on things on the earth, for ye are dead, and your life is hid with Christ in God.

NUMBERS 23 VS 19 to 23 God is not a man, that he should lie, neither the son of man, that he should repent; hath he said, and shall he not do it? Or hath he spoken, and shall he not make it good? Behold have received commandment to bless; and he hath blessed and I cannot reverse it.

When you know,
GOD BE IN US,
GOD BE WITH US,
GOD DWELLS IN US, GOD SHALL BE IN YOU,
TALK TO YOUR FUTURE WITH THE WORD OF GOD,
THAT'S WHAT GIVES YOU CONFIDENCE, KNOWING THAT YOU ARE NOT ALONE.
THE PROMISE OF GOD,

ISAIAH 40 VS 1 TO 5 Comfort ye. comfort ye my people, Saith your God. Speak ye comfortable to Jerusalem, and cry unto her, that her warfare is accomplished that her iniquity is pardoned; for she hath received of the Lord's hand double for all her sins. The voice of him that crieth in the wilderness. Prepare ye the way of the Lord, make straight in the desert a highway for the Lord. Every valley shall be exalted, every mountain and hill shall be made low, and the crooked shall be made straight, and the rough place plain; And the glory of the Lord shall be revealed and all flesh shall see it together; for the mouth of the Lord hath spoken it.

ZECHARAIAH 2 VS 5 TO 9 For l, saith the Lord, will be unto her a wall of fire round about, and will be the glory in the midst of her. Ho, ho, come forth, and flee from the land of the north, saith the Lord for I have spread, you abroad as the four winds of the heaven sent the Lord. Deliver thyself O Zion that dwellest with the daughter of Babylon, For thus saith the Lord of hosts; After the glory hath he sent me unto the nations which spoiled you; for he that toucheth you toucheth the apple of his eye. For, behold will shake mine hand upon them, and they shall be a spoil to their servants; and ye shall know that the Lord of hosts hath sent me.

NAHUM 1 VS 2 to 3 God is jealous; and the Lord revengeth; the Lord revengeth, and is furious, the Lord will take vengeance on his adversaries and he reserveth worth for his enemies. The Lord is slow to anger, and great in power, and will not at all acquit the wicked; the Lord hath his way in the whirlwind and in the storm, and the clouds are the dust of his feet.

# THE PROMISES OF GOD

PSALM 82 VS 6 I have said, Ye are gods; and all of you are children of most high. Amen.

PSALM 62 VS 5 to 6 My soul, wait thou only upon God; for my expectation is from him. He only is my rock and my salvation; he is my defence; I shall not be moved. I trust in him at all times; ye people, pour out your heart before him; God is a refuge for us Selah. Amen.

ISAIAH 3 VS 10 Say to the righteous, that it shall be well with him; for they shall eat the fruit of their doings. Amen.

EZEKIEL 36 VS 9 to 11 For behold I am you, and ye shall be tilled and sown; And I will multiply upon you man and beast; and they shall increase and bring fruit and settle you after your old estates; and will do better unto you than at your beginning and ye shall know that I am the Lord's. Amen.

PSALM 34 VS 5 They looked unto him; and were lightened and their faces were not ashamed. Amen.

2 PETER 1 VS 2 TO 4 Feed the flock of God which is among you, taking the oversight there of not by constraint, but willingly; not for filthy lucre, but of a ready mind; Whereby are giving unto us exceeding great and precious promises; that by these ye might be partakers of the divine nature having escaped the corruption that is in the world through lust.

Do you know that your mind is a stayed of God's word. He keeps it in perfect peace. Moreover, by the virtue of the divine life of Christ at work in us, we experience good health, property and victory. However, do you know that you are the expression of Godfullness and grace. And we manifest in His Kingdom and power. To God be the Glory.

2 PETER 3 VS 13 Nevertheless we, according to his promise, look for new heavens and a new earth, wherein dwelleth righteousness.

JAMES 1 VS 22 TO 24 But be ye doers of the word, and not hearers only, deceiving your own selves. For if any be a hearer of the word and not a doer; he is like unto a man beholding his natural face in a glass. For he beholdeth himself, and goeth his way, and straightway forgetteth what manner of man he was.

HEBREWS 13 VS 7 Remember them which have the rule over you, who have spoken unto you the word of God; whose faith follow, considering the end of their conversation.

2 JOHN 1 VS 2 For the truths, which dwelleth in us, and shall be with us forever.

JEREMIAH 30 VS 17 For I will restore health unto thee, and I will heal thee an Outcast, saying, This is Zion whom no man seeketh after.

2 TIMOTHY 3 VS 1 TO 5 Thou therefore, my son, be strong in the Lord in the grace that is in Christ Jesus. And the things that thou hast thou hast heard of me among many witnesses, the same commit to faithful men, who shall be able to teach others also. Thou therefore endure

hardness as a good soldier of Jesus Christ. No man that warreth entangleth himself with the affairs of this life; that he may please him who hath chose him to be a soldier. And if a man also strives for masteries, yet is he not crowned except he strives lawfully.

EPHESIANS 3 VS 16 to 19 That he would grant you, according to the riches of his glory, to be strengthened with might by his spirit in the inner man. That Christ may dwell in your hearts by faith; that ye, being rooted and grounded in love. May be able to comprehend with all saints what is the breadth, and length, and depth, and height. And to know the love of Christ, which passeth knowledge, that ye might be filled with all the fullness of God.

PHILIPPIANS 4 VS 6 to 7 Be careful for nothing; but in every thing by prayer and supplication with thanksgiving let your requests be made known unto God. And the peace of God, which passeth all understanding shall keep your hearts and minds through Christ Jesus. Finally, brethren whatsoever things are true, whatsoever things are honest, whatsoever things are pure, whatsoever things are just, whatsoever things are lovely, whatsoever things are of a good report; if there be any virtue and if there be any praise, think on these things. Those things which ye have both learned and received, and heard and seen in me, do and the God of peace shall be with you.

EPHESIANS 3 VS 10 Now unto him that is able to do exceeding abundantly above all that we ask or think, according to the power that worketh in us.

EPHESIANS 2 VS 4 to 7 But God, who is rich in mercy for his great love wherewith he loved us. Even when we were dead in sins, hath quickened us together with Christ, by grace you are saved. And hath raised us up together, and made us together in heavenly places the exceeding riches of his grace in his kindness toward us. Through Christ Jesus.

EPHESIANS 1 VS 3 Blessed be the God and the Father of our Lord Jesus Christ. Who hath blessed us with all spiritual blessings in heavenly places in Christ;

HAGGAI 2 VS 6 to 9 For thus saith the Lord of hosts; Yet once, it is a little while, and I will shake the heavens and the earth, and the sea, and the dry land; And I will shake all the nations, and the desire of all nations shall come; and I will fill this house with glory, saith the Lord of host. The glory of this latter house; and greater than the former, saith the Lord of hosts; and in this place will I give peace; saith the Lord of hosts. Amen.

ZEPHANIAN 3 VS 16 to 17 In that day it shall be said to Jerusalem. Fear thou not; and to Zion, let not thine hands be slack. The Lord thy God in the midst of thee is mighty, he will rejoice over thee with joy; he will rest in his love, he will joy over thee with singing.

PSALM 89 VS 8 to 9 O Lord of hosts, who is strong Lord like thee? Or to thy faithfulness round about thee? Thou rulest the raging of the sea; when the waves thereof arise, thou stillest them.

You need these verses in a time of trouble to pray with – best in the middle of the night:

PSALM 7 VS 6 to 10, PSALM 109 VS 13 to19, PSALM 74 VS 16 to 22, DANIEL 12 VS 2 to 4, PSALM 10 VS 9 to 15, PSALM 9 VS 7 to 20, PSALM 17 VS 9 to 19, PSALM 94 VS 1 to 7, PSALM 102 VS 13, PSALM 69 VS 1 to 6, PSALM 70 VS 1 to 5, PSALM 37 VS 23 to 24, JEREMIAH 33 VS 3, JOHN 2 VS 27 to 29, PROVERB 14 VS 12, PSALM 119 VS 133 to 143, CORINTHIANS 1 VS 5 to 7, DEUTER-ONOMY 30 VS 15, PROVERB 18 VS 20 to 15 to 21, PSALM 35 VS 1 to7, PSALM 27 VS 1 to 14, PSALM 59 VS 1 to 17, PSALM 91 VS 1 to 16.

May God hear our prayer. Amen.

# ACKNOWLEDGEMENT

Obviously, in a work of this nature, it is important to acknowledge the efforts of individuals, groups and family members without whom this work would not have been possible. May God bless you all. I thank God for my three sons for their support and caring, and my grandson, and pray that he will grow up to know that our family is blessed by God and is rooted in Christ; this following is our power and testament, crucified, raised, exalted and now residing in us. Moreover, I thank God for my family in Nigeria, always praying for me and letting me know that everything is going to be alright. That God is God of justice that no matter what happened, and have faith in Him, God almighty. Who never fails and never lies.

Lord, we realise that focusing on our troubles causes us to forget that even in the midst of trials, You are good. Teach us the way of a grateful heart. Thanksgiving is a virtue that grows through practice.

May God bless all who have read this book of encouragement. However, you know that all things work together for your good, to them that love God. Good or bad is for your good. Basically don't give up or give in, don't allow any obstacle to stop or discourage you, because out of every obstacle, there is a potential miracle.

> PSALM 62 VS 1 To 12 Truly my soul waiteth upon God from him cometh my salvation. He only is my rock and my salvation; he is my defence; I shall not be greatly moved. How long will ye imagine mischief against a man? ye shall be slain all of you; as a bowing wall shall ye be, and as a tottering fence. They only consult to cast him down from his excellency; they delight in lies; they bless with their mouth but they curse inwardly. Selah. My soul wait thou only upon God; for my expectation is from him. He only is my rock and my salvation he is my defence shall not be moved. In God is my salvation and my glory; the rock of my strength and my refuge is in God. Trust in him in all times; ye people pour out your heart before him. God is in refuge for us. Selah. Surely men of low degree are vanity, and men of high degree are a lie, to be laid in the balance; they are altogether higher than vanity.

Trust not in oppression and become not vain in robbery; if riches increase set not your heart upon them. God hath spoken once; and twice have I heard this that power belongeth unto God. Also, unto thee, O Lord, belongeth mercy; for thou renderest to every man according to his work.

PSALM 119 VS 10 to 16 With my whole heart have I sought thee; O let me not wonder from thy commandments. Hy word have I hid in mine heart, that I might not sin against thee. Blessed art thou, O Lord teach me thy statutes. With my lips have I declared all the judgments of thy mouth. I have rejoiced in the way of thy testimonies, as much as in all riches. I will meditate in thy precepts, and have respect unto thy ways. I will delight myself in thy statutes and will not forget thy word.

# USE THIS VERSE TO PRAY IN THE TIME OF TROUBLES

PSALM 140 VS 4 to 5 Keep me, O Lord, from the hands of the wicked man; preserve me from the violent man; who have purposed to overthrow my goings. The proud have hid a snare for me, and cords; they have spread a net by the wayside; they have set gins for me. Selah.

PSALM 144 VS 1 Blessed be the Lord my strength which teacheth my hands to war and my fingers to fight.

PSALM 119 VS 98 Thou through thy commandment hast made me wiser than mine enemies; for they are ever with me. I have more understanding than all my teachers for thy testimonies are my meditation.

NAHUM 3 VS 3 to 4 The horseman lifteth up both the bright sword and the glittering spear and there is a multimode of slain, and a great number of carcases and there is no end of their corpses and they stumble upon their corpses; Because of the multitude of the whoredoms of the well-favoured harlot, the mistress of witchcrafts.

HOSEA 9 VS 5 to 14 What will ye do in the solemn day, and in the day of the feast of the Lord? For, lo, they are gone because of Egypt shall gather them up, Memphis shall bury them; the pleasant places for their silver, nettles shall possess them; thorns shall be in their tubercles. The days of visitation are come, the days of recompense are come; Israel shall know it; the prophet is a fool, the spiritual man is mad, for the multitude of thine iniquity, and the great hatred. The watchman of Ephraim was with my God but the prophet is a snare of a fowler in all his ways, and hatred in the house of his God. They have deeply corrupted themselves, as in the days of Gibeah; therefore, he will remember their iniquity, he will visit their sins. I found Israel like grapes in the wilderness; I saw your fathers as the firstripe in the fig tree at her first time; but they went to Baal-peor, and separated themselves unto that shame, and their abominations were according as they loved. As for the Ephraim, their glory shall fly away like a bird from the birth and from the womb, and from the conception. Though they bring up their children, yet will I bereave them, that there shall not be a man left yea, woe also to them I depart from them. Ephraim, as I saw Tyrus, is planted in a pleasant place ;but Ephraim shall bring forth his children to the murderer. Give them Lord what wilt thou give? Give them a miscarrying womb and dry breasts.

JOB 5 VS 12 He disappointeth the devices of the crafty, so that their hands cannot perform their enterprise.

ISAIAH 44 VS 24 to25 Thus saith the Lord; thy redeemer and he that formed thee from the womb; I am the Lord that maketh all things that stretcheth forth the heavens alone; that spreadeth abroad the earth by myself. That frustrateth the takers of the liars, and maketh diviners mad; that turneth wise men backward, and maketh their knowledge foolish.

ISAIAH 54 VS 13 to 15 And all thy children shall be taught of the Lord; and great fall be the peace of thy children. In righteousness shalt be established; Thou shalt be far from oppression; for thou shalt not fear and from terror; for it shall not come near thee. Behold, they shall surely gather together; but not by me; whosoever shall gather together against thee shall fail for thy sake.

PSALM 45 VS 1 My heart is in a good matter speak of the things which I have made touching the King; my tongue is the pen of a ready writer.

ISAIAH 49 VS 25 to 26 But thus saith the Lord, Even the captive of the mighty shall be taken away; and the prey of the terrible shall be delivered; for I will contendeth with thee, and I will save thy children. And I will feed them that oppress thee with their own flesh; and they shall be drunken with their own blood, as with sweet wine; and all flesh shall know that I the Lord am thy Saviour and thy Redeemer, the mighty One of Jacob. Amen.

ROMANS 9 VS 14 to 16 What shall say then? Is there unrighteousness with God? God forbid. For he saith to Moses, I will have mercy on whom I will have mercy; and I will have compassion on whom I will have compassion. So then it is not of him that willeth, nor of him that runeth, but of God that sheweth mercy.

ISAIAH 33 VS 2 TO 3 O Lord be gracious unto us; we have waited for thee; be thou their arm every morning, our salvation also in the time of trouble. Amen.

ISAIAH 30 VS 13 and 15 to 18 Therefore this iniquity shall be to you as breach ready to fall, swelling out in a high wall whose breaking cometh suddenly at an instant. For thou saith the Lord God, the Holy One of Israel; In returning and rest shall ye be saved; in quietness and in confidence shall be your strength; and ye would not. But ye said, no for we will flee upon horses; therefore, shall ye flee; and. We will ride upon the swift; therefore, shall they that pursue you be swift. One thousand shall flee at the rebuke of one; at the rebuke of five shall ye flee ye be left as a beacon upon the top of a mountain, and as an ensign on an hill. And therefore, will the Lord want that he may be gracious unto you, and therefore will he be exalted that he may have mercy upon you; for the Lord is a God of judgment; blessed are all they that wait for him. For the people shall dwell in Zion at Jerusalem; thou shalt weep no more; he will be very gracious unto thee at the voice of thy cry; when he shall hear it. He will answer thee.

ISAIAH 33 VS 6 And wisdom and knowledge shall be the stability of thy times, and strength of Salvation; the fear of the Lord is his treasure. Enid Blyton

*"The best way to treat obstacles is to use them as stepping stones. Laugh at them, tread on them; and let them lead you to something better."*

**Will Smith**

*"A winner is a dreamer who never gives up."*

**Nelson Mandela**

Obviously, in life never apologise for who you are because your enemies see your potential before you realise who you are. Moreover, know the word of God in your spirit because it will help build you up and give you your inheritance.

Remember the poor, the needy, the stranger, the widow; when you help them, you are doing it for God. Moreover, nobody has seen God, but God sees us. Go to the motherless home and bless them too. Basically, look inside your family – they need help. Because charity begins at home. Actually, you should take care of your family and people close to you before you go about helping others. Moreover, it is better to give than to receive. Lord may we these days have eyes to see others' needs, and perceive direction from you on ways we might help, and the spirit to obey. May we live out the faith love and hope you have given us. Amen.

PSALM 41 VS 1 to 4 Blessed is he that considereth the poor; the Lord will deliver him in time of trouble. The Lord will preserve him and keep him alive; and he shall be blessed upon the earth and thou wilt not deliver him unto the will of his enemies. The Lord will strengthen him upon wilt make all his bed in his sickness. I said Lord, be merciful unto me heal my soul; for I have sinned against thee.

John D. Rockefeller said "I've made many millions but they brought me no real happiness. I'd barter them all for the days I sat on an office stool in Cleveland and counted myself rich on three dollars a week." Having more money may give you social status, but serving God gives your kingdom significance. Big difference! So, keep your focus on what matters.

Let us agree together in this word of God.

> EPHESIANS 1 VS 17 to 19 That the God of our Lord Christ, the Father of glory, may give unto you the spirit of wisdom and revelation in

the knowledge of him; The eyes of your understanding being enlightened; that ye may know what is the hope of his calling, and what the riches of his inheritance in the saints. And what is the exceeding greatness of his power towards us who believe, according to the working of his mighty power. Amen.

## Divine Health Confessions

My mind is stayed on God's word, therefore keeps me in perfect peace. By virtue of the divine life of Christ at work in us. I experience health, victory. And prosperity, now and always. I am the expression of God's fullness, grace, and glory manifest His Kingdom and power. Glory to God almighty. Hallelujah.

## DECISION PRAYER OF SALVATION

Will you accept Jesus as your saviour?

The Bible read, "if thou shall confess with thy mouth the Lord Jesus, and shall believe in thine heart that God hath raised Him from the dead, thou shall be saved. For with the heart man believeth unto righteousness and with the mouth confession is made unto salivation" **[ROMANS 10 VS 9 to 10]**

To receive Jesus as Lord and Saviour of your life, please pray this prayer from your heart today!

"Dear Jesus believe that you died for me and rose again on the third day. I confess I am a sinner need your love and forgiveness. Come in to my life, forgive my sins, and give me eternal life. I confess you as my Lord and my saviour. Thank you for my salvation, your peace and joy. Amen."

Congratulation if you said the salvation prayer, you are now born again and you have received Jesus's righteousness. Now study God's word and meditate on it day and night, believe it and what it says about you and see yourself that way and talk that way, even in time of opposition. Glory be to God.

> EXODUS 3 VS 21 And I will give this people favour in the sight of the Egyptians and it shall come to pass, that when ye go, ye shall not go empty. Amen.

## Divine Health Confessions

Blessing Father, thank you for the power in the Name of Jesus and authority I have to use the Name against the devil, sicknesses, diseases, and crises of life. I live healthily. I am triumphant and sustained by the power and authority of that Name. Today and always. Glory. Hallelujah!

If you need more information;
E-MAIL: vdaniels58@hotmail. com.
PHONE: 07711932865.

## *Also by Vivian Daniels:*

Coming to London -Crossing Over-
978-1-78222-081-7

Be Yourself
978-1-78222-093-0

Don't Give Up Your Hope in God
978-1-78222-451-8

Renew Your Mind
978-1-78222-610-9

Chill Out
978-1-78222-684-0

What's Up Trust God
978-1-78222-802-8

Milton Keynes UK
Ingram Content Group UK Ltd.
UKHW011819090224
437558UK00013B/507

9 781787 920439